THE POWER OF EMOTIONS

How to Manage Your Feelings and Overcome Negativity

By: Judy Dyer

THE POWER OF EMOTIONS:
How to Manage Your Feelings and Overcome Negativity
by Judy Dyer

© **Copyright 2021 by Judy Dyer**

All Rights Reserved.

ISBN: 979-8372614079

ALSO BY JUDY DYER

*Empath: A Complete Guide for Developing Your Gift
and Finding Your Sense of Self*

*The Empowered Empath: A Simple Guide on Setting Boundaries,
Controlling Your Emotions, and Making Life Easier*

*The Highly Sensitive: How to Stop Emotional Overload,
Relieve Anxiety, and Eliminate Negative Energy*

*Borderline Personality Disorder: A Complete BPD Guide for
Managing Your Emotions and Improving Your Relationships*

Empath and The Highly Sensitive: 2 in 1 Bundle

Empaths and Narcissists: 2 in 1 Bundle

CONTENTS

INTRODUCTION

Emotions are an important part of who we are, but they can be complicated, messy and confusing. Knowing how to name and articulate your emotions is essential to developing your emotional health. One of the main reasons why people find emotions so difficult to deal with is because they don't know how to manage them. If you were raised in a household where children were seen and not heard and emotional regulation was not a topic of conversation, there is a good chance you have been emotionally stunted and find it difficult to deal with negative emotions. Do you shut down, run away or lash out when you get uncomfortable with how you feel? If you answered yes to this question, the information in this book will empower you to start taking control of your emotional health. I can say this with confidence because no more than 8 years ago, I was exactly where you are today. Let me tell you a bit about myself.

I was raised in a middle-class home with very old-fashioned parents. I love my parents more than anything, and they equipped me with many of the life skills I have today. I was raised to be respectful, to have manners and etiquette, and education was a very important part of our household. But emotional regulation was the missing part of the jigsaw. My parents were raised in an era when children did what they were told, and any questions asked or defiance shown was met with a belt. They learned very quickly to put up and shut up, that making a fuss about anything simply wasn't an option. When they were angry or frustrated, they were put in time out. When they cried because they were being bullied, they were told to wipe their eyes and go to bed. The only time they had the right to be upset was if they were physically injured. A cut knee, or a sprained ankle was rewarded with candy, warm milk or a trip to the toy store. They raised my siblings and me the same way, and as a result, we learned to repress our emotions, and this habit showed up in my adult relationships.

I have been married and divorced twice; my first marriage lasted six months, my second, one year and three months. I have now been married for five years and I believe this time, it will last forever. My first two marriages broke down because neither I nor my then-husbands knew how to regulate our emotions. When we experienced emotional challenges, we didn't know how to handle them, so we walked away. I have lost many friends for the same reason.

After my second marriage, I got terribly depressed because I believed my partners and my friends left because there was something wrong with me. When I hit rock bottom, I went to see a therapist, and it was during this time I learned that all my problems stemmed from trapped emotions, and my inability to manage my feelings because of how I was raised. My therapist was amazing, patient and understanding. She worked with me for several years and gave me plenty of strategies for managing my emotions. Today, I am much better, I feel better and my relationships are better.

Emotional wellbeing has been underestimated for decades. But the reality is that modern life is loaded with emotional challenges. The desire for career satisfaction, good relationships and success, along with the fear of missing out, and the pressure to keep up with the Joneses can all conjure up erratic combinations of emotions. Unfortunately, society doesn't teach us how to work with our emotions, it teaches us to avoid and block them, and we seem to do this quite well. Between prescription drug use, alcohol use, screen time and working excessively long hours, we have mastered the art of avoiding our emotions. But it's not healthy and I would go as far as to say that an unhealthy emotional state is worse than an unhealthy diet. Here's why:

- It contributes to some of the deadliest diseases and conditions such as type-2 diabetes, cancer, heart disease and dementia.
- It leads to anxiety, depression and a host of other psychological disorders.
- It leads people to feel isolated and misunderstood.

The good news is that you can learn to connect with your negative emotions and use them to your advantage. If you are ready to gain control of your emotional health and overcome negative feelings, the strategies and the information in this book are exactly what you need.

In order to maximize the value you receive from this book, I highly encourage you to join our tight-knit community on Facebook. Here you will be able to connect and share with others in order to continue your growth.

Taking this journey alone is not recommended, and this can be an excellent support network for you.

It would be great to connect with you there,

Judy Dyer

To Join, Visit:

www.pristinepublish.com/empathgroup

DOWNLOAD THE AUDIO VERSION OF THIS BOOK FREE

If you love listening to audiobooks on the go or would enjoy a narration as you read along, I have great news for you. You can download the audiobook version of *The Power of Emotions* for FREE just by signing up for a FREE 30-day Audible trial!

Visit: www.pristinepublish.com/audiobooks

YOUR FREE GIFT - HEYOKA EMPATH

A lot of empaths feel trapped, as if they've hit a glass ceiling they can't penetrate. They know there's another level to their gift, but they can't seem to figure out what it is. They've read dozens of books, been to counselling, and confided in other experienced empaths, but that glass ceiling remains. They feel alone, and alienated from the rest of the world because they know they've got so much more to give, but can't access it. Does this sound like you?

The inability to connect to your true and authentic self is a tragedy. Being robbed of the joy of embracing the full extent of your humanity is a terrible misfortune. The driving force of human nature is to live according to one's own sense of self, values, and emotions. Since the beginning of time, philosophers, writers, and scholars have argued that authenticity is one of the most important elements of an individual's well-being.

When there's a disconnect between a person's inner being and their expressions, it can be psychologically damaging. Heyokas are the most powerful type of empaths, and many of them are not fully aware of who they are. While other empaths experience feelings of overwhelm and exhaustion from absorbing others' energy and emotions, heyoka empaths experience an additional aspect of exhaustion in that they are fighting a constant battle with their inability to be completely authentic.

The good news is that the only thing stopping you from becoming your authentic self is a lack of knowledge. You need to know exactly who you are so you can tap into the resources that have been lying dormant within you. In this bonus e-book, you'll gain in-depth information about the seven signs that you're a heyoka empath, and why certain related abilities are such powerful traits. You'll find many of the answers to the questions you've been searching for your entire life such as:

- Why you feel uncomfortable when you're around certain people
- How you always seem to find yourself on the right path even though your decisions are not based on logic or rationale
- The reason you get so offended when you find out others have lied to you
- Why you analyze everything in such detail
- The reason why humor is such an important part of your life
- Why you refuse to follow the crowd, regardless of the consequences
- The reason why strangers and animals are drawn to you

There are three main components to authenticity: understanding who you are, expressing who you are, and letting the world experience who you are. Your first step on this journey is to know who you are, and with these seven signs that you're a heyoka empath, you'll find out. I've included snippets about the first three signs in this description to give you full confidence that you're on the right track:

Sign 1: You Feel and Understand Energy

Heyoka empaths possess a natural ability to tap into energy. They can walk into a room and immediately discern the atmosphere. When an individual walks past them, they can literally see into their soul because they can sense the aura that person is carrying. But empaths also understand their own energy, and they allow it to guide them. You will often hear this ability referred to as "the sixth sense." The general consensus is that only a few people have this gift. But the reality is that everyone was born with the ability to feel energy; it's just been demonized and turned into something spooky, when in actual fact, it's the most natural state to operate in.

Sign 2: You are Led by Your Intuition

Do you find that you just know things? You don't spend hours, days, and weeks agonizing over decisions, you can just feel that something is the right thing to do, and you go ahead and do it. That's because you're led by your intuition and you're connected to the deepest part of yourself. You know your soul, you listen to it, and you trust it. People like Oprah Winfrey, Steve Jobs and Richard Branson followed their intuition steadfastly and it led them to become some of the most successful people in the history of the world. Living from within is the way we were created to be, and those who trust this ability will find their footing in life a lot more quickly than others. Think of it as a GPS system: when it's been programmed properly, it will always take you to your destination via the fastest route.

Sign 3: You Believe in Complete Honesty

In general, empaths don't like being around negative energy, and there's nothing that can shift a positive frequency faster than dishonesty. Anything that isn't the truth is a lie, even the tiny ones that we excuse away as "white lies." And as soon as they're released from someone's mouth, so is negative energy. Living an authentic life requires complete honesty at all times, and although the truth may hurt, it's better than not being able to trust someone. Heyoka empaths get very uncomfortable in the presence of liars. They are fully aware that the vibrations of the person don't match the words they are saying. Have you ever experienced a brain freeze mid-conversation? All of a sudden you just couldn't think straight, you couldn't articulate yourself properly, and things just got really awkward? That's because your empath antenna picked up on a lie.

Heyoka Empath: 7 Signs You're A Heyoka Empath & Why It's So Powerful is a revolutionary tool that will help you transition from uncertainty to complete confidence in who you are. In this easy-to-read guide, I will walk you through exactly what makes you a heyoka empath. I've done the research for you, so no more spending hours, days, weeks, and even years searching for answers, because everything you need is right here in this book.

You have a deep need to share yourself with the world, but you've been too afraid because you knew something was missing. The information within the pages of this book is the missing piece in the jigsaw puzzle of your life. There's no turning back now!

Get *Heyoka Empath* for Free by Visiting

www.pristinepublish.com/empathbonus

CHAPTER 1

WHAT ARE EMOTIONS?

Our emotions determine how we feel, how we treat ourselves and how we relate to others. Most people are reactionary; they are governed by their emotions and whatever they feel, they express. According to experts, emotions are a universal language. A native American can tell that a Chinese person is angry even if they can't understand the words they are speaking. The tone of voice and body language will let them know. Psychologist Paul Ekman began studying emotions in the 1970s, and he found that there were six basic universal emotions: happiness, sadness, anger, disgust, surprise and fear. But a 2017 study published in the *Proceedings of the National Academy of Sciences* reported 27 different categories of emotion. I will mention them briefly. But for the purpose of this book, in this chapter, I will focus on the six basic universal emotions highlighted by Paul Ekman.

HAPPINESS

Everyone desires to be happy because it feels good. It is an emotional state characterized by feelings of wellbeing, satisfaction, gratification, joy and contentment. Happiness is typically expressed through:

- Smiling
- A relaxed posture
- A pleasant and upbeat way of speaking

Although happiness is experienced worldwide, what we desire to make us happy differs among cultures. For example, in many Western countries, society promotes that you need to live a certain lifestyle in order to be happy. A nice house, an expensive car, plenty of material possessions and an attractive partner make you happy. In Kenya, the Maasai tribe values cows, so they are a great source of pride for members of the tribe. They live in small huts and have no desire for the material wealth required for happiness in the West. Additionally, regardless of culture, the things that contribute to a state of happiness are a lot more complex and highly individualized. For example, many rich and famous people commit suicide. The response to such deaths is typically, "Why would those who have everything society says you need to live a fulfilling life kill themselves?" Again, it's because there is much more to happiness than cultural ideologies or financial success.

SADNESS

Sadness is a transient emotion characterized by feelings of disinterest, hopelessness, grief, disappointment and low mood. In general, people don't experience sadness often. Those who go through prolonged periods of severe sadness are sometimes diagnosed with depression. Sadness is typically expressed by:

- Withdrawal
- Crying
- Quietness

- Lethargy
- Dampened mood

The severity and type of sadness will vary depending on the reason behind the emotion. Additionally, the way people cope with sadness can differ as well. Some people deal with it by thinking negative thoughts, self-medicating and avoiding people.

ANGER

Anger is a very powerful emotion characterized by feelings of antagonism, frustration, agitation and hostility. Anger can play a role in the body's *fight or flight* response. When a threat makes you feel angry, you will want to protect yourself and fight off the danger. It is often expressed through the following:

- Aggressive behavior such as kicking, hitting or throwing objects
- Physiological responses such as turning red or sweating
- Tone of voice changes such as shouting
- Body language, such as folding the arms, or clenching fists
- Facial expressions such as glaring or frowning

Anger can become very destructive when it isn't managed properly and turns into rage. However, it can also be used as a source of motivation for change (I will discuss this further in Chapter 6).

FEAR

Like anger, fear triggers the fight or flight response. When we think we are in danger, several biological changes take place in the body that enable us to fight or run. The heart rate increases, the muscles tense up, more blood starts pumping through the body and the mind becomes more alert. This response protects us from danger because it allows us to react accordingly. Fear is generally expressed through the following:

- Wide, darting eyes
- Running or hiding
- Quickened heartbeat, rapid breathing

We can also develop these reactions to anticipated threats that have not taken place, but which we imagine are going to happen. Fear of this kind is referred to as anxiety. Many people suffer from social anxiety, meaning they are afraid of engaging in social situations. On the flip side, there are some people who enjoy fear and seek out activities that will invoke fear, such as extreme sports.

DISGUST

Disgust is a sense of revulsion that manifests because of a number of things such as an unpleasant smell, sight, taste, or something that someone has said or done. Research suggests that the emotion of disgust emerged as a way of protecting the body against anything harmful. Disgust is expressed in a number of ways:

- Refusing to look at the thing that disgusts you
- Retching or vomiting
- Curling the upper lip, or wrinkling the nose

SURPRISE

Surprise is a brief response occurring when a person is startled by something unexpected. Whether the emotion is positive or negative depends on the situation. For example, if your friend throws you a surprise party, you are going to be pleasantly surprised. But if that same friend jumps out from the closet when you come home from work, you will be surprised, but it won't be pleasant. Surprise is typically expressed through the following:

- Opening the mouth, widening the eyes, raising the eyebrows
- Gasping, screaming or yelling
- Jumping back

Surprise can also trigger the fight or flight response; it is common for people to either freeze or run when they are surprised.

As we all know, there are many more than the six basic emotions described by Ekman. In his later research, he added several other emotions, but suggested that unlike the original emotions, they were not always recognized through facial expressions. These emotions include:

- Shame
- Satisfaction
- Relief
- Pride in achievement
- Guilt
- Excitement
- Embarrassment
- Contentment
- Contempt
- Amusement

DIFFERENT THEORIES ON EMOTIONS

Over the years, several theories have emerged about emotions and many psychologists disagree with the emotional classifications established by Ekman. For example, Dr. Rachael Jack argues that there are only four basic emotions. Others have put forward that emotions exist in a hierarchical form. For example, primary emotions include joy, love, sadness, anger and surprise, but they can be broken down even further into secondary emotions. For example, love is also made up of secondary emotions such as longing and affection. These secondary emotions can then be broken down into tertiary emotions such as tenderness, compassion, caring and liking.

A 2017 study conducted by New York University and published in the *Proceedings of the National Academy of Science* journal claims that there are a minimum of 27 distinct emotions that include: surprise, sexual desire, satisfaction, sadness, romance, relief, nostalgia, joy, interest, horror, fear, excitement, entrancement, empathic pain, disgust, craving, confusion, calmness, boredom, awkwardness, awe, anxiety, anger, amusement, appreciation, aesthetic emotion, adoration and admiration. Researchers in the study put forward the idea that a better clarification of emotions will help physicians, psychologists and scientists learn more about the role emotions play in brain activity, mood and behavior. Additionally, a better understanding of these emotional states will help experts develop better treatments for psychiatric conditions.

THE MAKEUP OF AN EMOTION

To further understand emotions, there are three key elements to consider: the subjective experience, the physiological response and the behavioral response.

THE SUBJECTIVE RESPONSE

As you have read, Paul Eckman believes there are six basic universal emotions experienced worldwide, regardless of culture or background. Experts also believe that there is a subjective element to emotions. For example, anger is not all the same; you will know from your own experience that you can feel anything from a hint of anger or slight annoyance to burning rage. In other words, these broad labels cover diverse ground that is a lot more multi-dimensional.

It is also important to mention that our emotions are sometimes mixed. For example, when you are moving to a different country, you might be nervous and excited at the same time. Giving birth or getting married can conjure up a variety of emotions such as anxiety, fear, joy and anticipation. These emotions might take place at the same time, or one after the other in succession.

THE PHYSIOLOGICAL RESPONSE

There is also a very real psychological element to emotions. Fear can cause the heart to beat so fast you can hear it. Anxiety can cause you to feel sick, and in some cases, you may even throw up. According to the Cannon Bard theory, we feel emotions and psychological reactions at the same time. Physiological responses such as a racing heartbeat and sweaty palms are regulated by a part of the automatic nervous system called the sympathetic nervous system.

The automatic nervous system is responsible for the bodily functions we don't consciously control such as digestion and blood flow. The sympathetic nervous system activates the fight or flight response. Traditionally, research on the physiology of emotions focused on these autonomic responses. However, this focus has shifted to the role that the brain plays in emotions. Brain scans highlight the fact that a part of the limbic system called the amygdala plays an important role in emotion, especially fear.

The amygdala is a tiny structure shaped like an almond; brain imaging studies have found that when people are exposed to threatening images, the amygdala is activated. Research also suggests that damage to the amygdala causes an impairment to the fear response.

THE BEHAVIORAL RESPONSE

Everyone can relate to behavioral responses because you have either experienced them yourself, or you've witnessed the reaction in someone else. The behavioral response is about how emotions are expressed. I find the behaviroal response particularly interesting because I am always intrigued at how wrong people get it. For example, there have been several times when I've been in a fantastic mood, but because I didn't have a wide smile on my face, people would walk up to me in the street and tell me to smile. It seems like an indirect way of telling me I look miserable. According to psychologists, these people are lacking in emotional intelligence, because our level of emotional intelligence determines how well we read other people (I will discuss this shortly). There are several factors that determine how we interpret and express emotions, and sociocultural norms is one of them. For example, in Japan, when an authority figure is present, people mask displays of disgust and fear. The Japanese are also more likely to express negative emotions alone.

EMOTIONS AND MOOD

It is also important to mention that emotions and moods are not the same, even though they are often referred to interchangeably. According to psychologists, the main distinction between the two is timing. Emotions are typically very intense but short lived. Emotions are also more likely to have an identifiable and definite cause. For example, you might get frustrated because the bus —driver drove off without you despite the fact that he saw you running towards the bus stop. But this frustration will probably only last for a couple of minutes at the most, especially if you get distracted by something else such as a phone call. However, a mood lasts longer than an emotion despite the fact that it is milder. There are also times when you can't identify the cause of the mood. For example, you may all of a sudden start feeling miserable for no reason. You haven't had an argument with anyone, you haven't watched a depressing movie, you literally just woke up feeling fed up.

EMOTIONAL INTELLIGENCE

We all know that one person who is always cool, calm and collected. They have a special ability to deal with really awkward social situations, and they instinctively know how to make people feel comfortable. People with this nature have high emotional intelligence (EQ). Emotional intelligence refers to the skill of managing and understanding emotions. According to psychologists, EQ plays an important role in success, and some argue that it is even more important than intelligence. Nevertheless, emotional intelligence is related to things such as academic achievement and decision making. Psychologist Daniel Goleman is the pioneer of emotional intelligence and he identifies the following five components to this skill:

Self-Awareness

It starts with the self; basically, if you are unable to understand yourself, you will find it very difficult to understand others. Self-awareness is the most important aspect of emotional intelligence because it gives you the ability to understand how your emotions, moods and actions affect others. Self-awareness requires you to evaluate your own emotions, recognize the emotional reactions in others, and then identify the underlying emotion. Additionally, self-awareness means that you understand the strong relationship between feelings and behavior.

Self-awareness also means that you are able to recognize your own strengths and weaknesses, you are open to new experiences and information, and you learn from the people you interact with. Goleman states that self-aware individuals are light-hearted, with a good sense of humor; they are confident in who they are and their abilities, and they are aware of how they are perceived by others.

Self-Regulation

Emotional regulation and management is a key component in emotional intelligence. This doesn't mean that you bury how you really feel, but it does mean that you wait for the right time and place to express it. For example, you can safely assume that the man who lashes out at his partner during the family dinner has low emotional intelligence. Self-regulation is about expressing your emotions in the right way.

Self-regulated people are flexible, and they don't have a problem adapting to change. Furthermore, they are good at calming down difficult or tense situations and managing conflict. Self-regulated people are also extremely conscientious.

They take responsibility for their actions and they are careful about the influence they have over others.

SOCIAL SKILLS

Emotionally intelligent people possess very good social skills. They have a powerful ability to mingle and communicate with everyone effectively. They can build strong relationships quickly. One of the main reasons for this is that emotionally intelligent people make those they are engaging with feel understood. Emotional understanding is about putting the information you have about the emotions of others to work as you interact with people throughout the day.

In a professional environment, this skill is massively important to managers because it allows them to build connections and relationships with employees. Employees benefit from being able to build strong relationships with their co-workers and superiors. Essential social skills include effective verbal and nonverbal communication skills, active listening skills and persuasion and leadership skills.

EMPATHY

Empathy is one of the key elements of emotional intelligence because it involves the ability to understand things from other people's perspectives. It means not just being able to recognize a person's emotional state, but also being able to step into that person's shoes and respond accordingly.

The ability to empathize with others also allows us to gain insight into the power dynamics in a social setting. Empathetic people can determine how these dynamics influence relation-ships, behaviors and feelings.

INTRINSIC MOTIVATION

Intrinsic motivation involves being motivated beyond external rewards such as acclaim, recognition, money, and fame. People with this skill have a passion for improving the lives of others. They are dedicated to fulfilling personal goals because they know that it is only by becoming the best version of themselves that they will have enough energy and goodwill to pour into the lives of others. Such people are goal oriented, committed and have a strong desire to succeed in everything they do.

Now you have a better understanding of emotions, both positive and negative, how they manifest and what makes up an emotion. In the next chapter, you will learn how negative emotions can work against you.

CHAPTER 2

HOW NEGATIVE EMOTIONS CAN WORK AGAINST YOU

Negative emotions are the ones that don't feel good. Since it's only natural that we don't want to feel bad, we avoid negative emotions. Negative emotions include but are not limited to anger, jealousy, sadness, a sense of failure, resentment, overwhelm, depression, loneliness, guilt, fear, helplessness, inadequacy, frustration and emptiness. All emotions are natural, they are what make us human, and there is nothing wrong with expressing positive or negative emotions. The problem is that a lot of people were raised in households where there was no regulation of emotions.

I was raised in a household where children were to be seen and not heard. There was no such thing as emotional management in my house. All negative emotions were immediately snuffed out by my parents with words such as, *"Stop being silly,"* or *"You are overreacting."* It was even worse for my brothers because for them, crying was seen as a sign of weakness. My dad would say things to them like, *"Man up, boys don't cry in this house"* or *"Crying is for girls."* As a result, we all grew up suppressing our emotions and incapable of communicating our feelings because we were afraid of being judged. We carried that fear with us into our adult lives, and buried feelings such as frustration, sadness and anger. When you are raised in an environment where you are reprimanded for expressing your feelings, whether positive or negative, you lose confidence. When someone is constantly shutting down your feelings, you are made to feel insignificant. Feelings of insignificance become a part of your subconscious programming and unbeknownst to you, become the driving force behind your life.

NEGATIVE EMOTIONS AND THE RIPPLE EFFECT

It's 2:00 am, you are in bed but awake, eyes fixed on the ceiling, worrying about the problems you are currently facing. You are in such a heightened state of anxiety that you just can't sleep. Yet, the following day, when a friend asks how things are going, your response is, *"yeah… great,"* but what you really feel is immense sadness. The distraction and pressure is so intense that the last thing on your mind is going to the gym. Instead, you roll out of bed an hour before work, stop off at the McDonalds drive through for breakfast, despite the fact that you're struggling to pay the bills. You're too stressed to think about cooking dinner, so you order Chinese on the way back from work. You wash that down with a beer, sit in front of the TV until bedtime and the vicious cycle starts again the next day.

Can you see the connection here? Your bad emotional health is destroying your physical health. It is important to re-member that our emotions are linked to physiological reactions in the brain. Every emotion triggers the release of hormones and chemicals that affect our physical health. Let's take a look at what the chemical cortisol does to the body:

THE CORTISOL EFFECT

When you confront something startling or threatening such as a near accident, or a call that your child has been injured, you feel a surge of energy. When your body experiences stress, cortisol (also known as the stress hormone) is released into the bloodstream. It causes your blood pressure and heart rate to increase. It is the body's natural response to threats, known as the 'fight or flight' response. Cortisol is also released during exercise and when you wake up in the morning. Normal cortisol levels help regulate blood sugar and blood pressure. Cortisol also assists in strengthening the heart, lowering pain sensitivity, boosting the immune system and improving memory.

How Cortisol Works: Once cortisol has been released into the bloodstream, glucose floods the body which provides energy for the large muscles. It also restricts the production of insulin so that glucose is available for immediate use. The hormone epinephrine speeds up the heart rate, and cortisol narrows the arteries. Both functions work together to increase the rate at which blood is pumped around the body as you handle the threat you are facing. Once the threat has passed, your hormone levels return to normal.

However, a combination of suppressed emotions, and the fast-paced lives we currently live, keeps the body in a high stress mode which can cause unpleasant symptoms such as:

Digestive Problems: When the body reacts to a threat, other less important functions such as digestion are inhibited. When your body is in a constant state of high alert, the digestive tract is unable to absorb or digest food properly.

Conditions such as ulcers, irritable bowel syndrome and colitis are all related to a deficient digestive system.

Reduced Immune System: One of the benefits of cortisol is that it lowers inflammation in the body. However, if cortisol levels are too high for too long it can supress the immune system. A suppressed immune system increases your risk of contagious illnesses, allergies, autoimmune diseases and cancer.

Weight Gain: When the cells are crying out for energy, that can give the body false hunger signals and cause you to overeat. Studies have found a connection between calorie intake and cortisol levels. The more cortisol in the system, the more calories you will want to eat.

High Blood Sugar: Insulin helps the cells turn glucose into energy. When the pancreas is struggling to keep the up with the body's need for insulin, the result is an excess of glucose, and the cells are starved of the sugar they need to function effectively.

NEGATIVE EMOTIONS AFFECT HEART HEALTH

How often have you said the words, *"It broke my heart," "I was scared to death,"* or *"You almost gave me a heart attack."* We repeat sayings like this because whether we are consciously aware of it or not, there is an intimate connection between the heart and mind. Negative emotions such as chronic stress, anger, loneliness, anxiety and depression are first formed in the mind. They all increase the risk of heart disease or put additional pressure on pre-existing heart conditions. There are several conditions that are caused by negative emotions:

Broken Heart Syndrome: Broken heart syndrome is also referred to as cardiomyopathy, apical ballooning syndrome and takotsubo cardiomyopathy. It is a temporary heart condition that people experience as a result of extremely stressful life events and strong negative emotions. People suffering from the condition may think they are having a heart attack because of the sudden chest pains that it causes due to an interruption in the way the heart pumps. The heart will also start having forceful contractions. The symptoms are typically reversed after a few days or weeks. However, if the pains are persistent, you are experiencing shortness of breath, or a rapid or irregular heartbeat, call 911.

Experts believe that excess amounts of stress hormones like adrenaline may have a negative effect on some people. It is also suspected that a temporary obstruction of the small or large arteries may damage the heart. Broken heart syndrome is typically experienced immediately after an intense emotional event such as:

- Divorce
- Financial difficulty or job loss
- A difficult argument
- Domestic abuse
- A life-threatening medical diagnosis
- A loved one's death

In a very few cases, broken heart syndrome can cause death. However, most people recover quickly and don't experience any long-term side effects. Additional rare complications include:

- Heart failure
- Heartbeat disruptions
- Low blood pressure
- Backup fluid in the lungs

Unforgiveness and Healing: In 1978, burns specialist surgeon Dr. Dabney Ewin was on duty at a New Orleans emergency room. He was assigned to a burn victim, an employee at the Kaiser Aluminium Plant who had fallen up to his knees into a vat of molten aluminium at a temperature of 950 degrees. He was in such agonizing pain that Dr. Ewin used his hypnotic training to put him into a state of 'induction.' This is an unconventional practice, and you will rarely find a doctor using it, however, this was a desperate situation. Burns of that magnitude typically require multiple skin grafts and take months to heal. In some cases, amputation is required. But because of the hypnosis sessions, the patient completely healed within eighteen days without any type of surgery.

His speedy recovery gave Dr. Ewin the confidence to keep using hypnosis on burn victims. He added another element, and that was to talk to his patients about anger and forgiveness. He found that many of his burn victims were extremely angry. Their burns were often due to their own actions or the actions of others. Dr. Ewin went on to explain that when describing what happened to them, they spoke with venom, frustration and anger. Dr. Ewin concluded that these negative feelings acted as a barrier to their healing. They were unable to relax, and their focus seemed to be on getting revenge rather than getting better. Extreme feelings of anger had a particularly negative effect on skin grafts because the body would reject them. When Dr. Ewin detected unforgiveness or anger in his patients, under hypnosis, he would take them through the process of forgiveness.

Dr. Ewin has taught other burn surgeons and colleagues his hypnosis techniques to induce forgiveness, and they have all had massive success. He has received thousands of letters worldwide thanking him for teaching them about the miracle of forgiveness.

Today, medical books classify unforgiveness as a disease. According to Dr. Steven Standiford, it causes sickness and keeps people sick. It is such a hindering and destructive force that forgiveness therapy is administered in the treatment of fatally ill cancer patients. Experts agree that emotional issues make it difficult for patients to respond well to medication. During the research phase for his book *The Forgiveness Project,* Dr. Michael Barry discovered that 61 percent of participants suffering from cancer were holding a grudge against someone and were unable to forgive them. Continuous feelings of anger and resentment lead to chronic anxiety which means there is an excess of cortisol and adrenaline flowing through the body. As a result, the immune system is unable to produce the cells required to fight cancer.

Many negative emotions are difficult to overcome because we encountered them during childhood and they were left unresolved. In Chapter 3, you will gain a better understanding of how these emotional wounds have kept you stuck during adulthood.

EMOTIONAL WOUNDS FROM CHILDHOOD THAT KEEP YOU STUCK DURING ADULTHOOD

The family is meant to be a safe and loving environment. Children should feel more than comfortable going to their parents and speaking about the things that are causing them emotional distress. However, in many cases, the family is the source of emotional pain and some children are severely damaged because of the way they were raised. If you can relate to this, know it's never too late to heal; but first, let's take a look at some of the emotional wounds from childhood that can have a negative effect on your adult life.

A Lack of Affection: When a child doesn't get love, affection and support from their parents, they end up feeling isolated and inadequate. A lack of affection also leads to co-dependency and an unhealthy desire for attention. The constant need for approval is the root cause of people pleasing. People pleasers invest all their time and energy trying to make other people happy just so they can hear something positive said about them. What typically happens to people pleasers is that they get so lost in taking care of everyone else that they forget to take care of themselves. Eventually, bitterness sets in because they don't get the recognition they feel they deserve for the amount of effort they've put in. People pleasers don't understand what self-confidence and self-love is because they are totally dependent on outside validation.

When you are constantly seeking validation from others, it is impossible to live a happy and fulfilling life because your feelings will always depend on someone else's opinion of you.

Abandonment or Neglect: If you were abandoned or neglected by your parents/caregivers as a child it can cause passive behavior. Children who experience neglect or abandonment believe they must have done something wrong for the people who are meant to love them to leave them. One of the many consequences of this belief is that the child will suppress emotions such as anger or hurt out of fear that it will cause them to be neglected or abandoned again. As a result, the child no longer acknowledges their feelings, and they end up being passive during adulthood. Passive adults never live up to their full potential because they are too afraid to go for what they want in case they are neglected or abandoned. For example, the passive adult is well aware they need to study three hours a night to pass their exams, but they won't do it because they have been paralyzed by the fear they refuse to acknowledge.

The False Self: When children are abused whether physically, emotionally or mentally, one of their defense mechanisms is to create a 'false self.' The false self is a character they adopt to protect themselves from abuse. Such children might become overly happy and cheerful when they are around people because they believe their parents will treat them better if they change their behavior. As a result, in adulthood, they keep that mask on. You might be this person or know someone who is this person… they are happy and bubbly all the time. People love being around them because they seem so positive. But deep down, they are terribly depressed, they live their life in fear of expressing difficult emotions because they are terrified of being rejected.

Co-dependency: Some children are forced into adulthood before their time. They may have had a sick brother or sister, a sick parent or they were raised by a single mother who kept having children, so they were given adult responsibilities such as cooking and cleaning. Children whose parents are co-dependent on them grow up believing that love is conditional. Co-dependent parents indirectly teach their children that the only time they receive any type of positive attention from their parents is when they please them by doing exactly what they say. For example, a child with a sick mother will be called up and down the stairs several times a day to run various errands. If the child doesn't arrive within seconds of being called, they get scolded; if the food isn't cooked to perfection, they get scolded; if they miss one item on the shopping list, they get scolded. The only time the child is shown any love is when the mother is satisfied that the task has been performed to her standard. During adulthood, children who were raised in such an environment become co-dependent and typically end up in abusive relationships.

The notion of conditional love creates a trauma bond with the parent. When a child is praised and told that they are amazing for doing the right thing, dopamine, oxytocin and serotonin are released and the child feels happy that they are loved. When they are screamed at for 'getting it wrong' and told they are 'useless' and 'stupid,' they feel sad. Their parent or caregiver takes them on a constant emotional rollercoaster and their lives are spent trying to please their parents. During adulthood, this behavior continues. One of the many wounds from this type of upbringing is low self-esteem. Therefore, as adults, they don't believe they are worthy of true love. These limited beliefs generally attract the wrong people, and the abuser then treats them the same way their parents did. Praise them when they get it right, insult or physically abuse them when they get it wrong. The victim is constantly trying to win their approval to hear the praise that they craved during childhood.

What's the Solution?

The first step in emotional healing is acceptance; many people are unaware of unresolved emotional trauma in their life because they have become experts at masking it. The man who works 80 hours a week, provides all the material benefits to his children but shows them no love, does so because he is emotionally unavailable. In most cases, he is emotionally unavailable because of unresolved childhood trauma. The woman in a relationship who dumps her partner as soon as she develops feelings for them does so because she was raised in an environment where any display of emotion was criticized. As an adult, her emotions make her feel so uncomfortable that she abandons relationships as soon as she develops feelings.

If you feel that you possess any of the characteristics mentioned above, healing is possible. In the next few chapters, you will learn how to overcome those challenges.

CHAPTER 4

EMOTIONAL NUMBNESS AND HOW TO OVERCOME IT

"You need to grow thicker skin," "you're such a cry baby," "just get over it, it's not that serious," and "boys don't cry." We have all heard these phrases at some point in our lives, and the person who said them probably wasn't trying to cause long lasting damage, they were probably just repeating what their parents, siblings or friends once said to them. Unfortunately, these words are confirmation of one of the many tragic truths we live with in this world: that expressing your negative emotions is a sign of weakness. If you were born into a family that didn't allow you to express your feelings, or a culture in which the foundation of masculinity is repressed emotions, there is a good chance that you suffer from emotional numbness. You may have experienced a traumatic life event such as the death of a loved one, a car accident or a divorce. The emotions that can surface from such events are so overwhelming that people repress them instead of facing them head on. Emotional numbness is detrimental to your mental wellbeing and it's really important that you overcome it.

EMOTIONAL NUMBNESS – WHAT IS IT?

When the mind is exposed to intense emotions, it employs a defense mechanism to protect itself. The mind trains itself to avoid emotions such as grief, jealousy, hatred and fear. When you experience emotional numbness, you lose the ability to experience and feel your emotions on an emotional and psychological level. Experts believe there is a strong connection between dissociation and emotional numbness. Dissociation is when a person disconnects from their senses, body, environment, identity and memories.

EMOTIONAL NUMBNESS – THE CAUSE

Emotional numbness is rooted in childhood trauma. You might be thinking, *"Well, I didn't have a traumatic childhood, my parents were fantastic."* You might have been given all the tools to succeed in life apart from emotional intelligence. A lot of people make excellent parents in some areas, but not in others, and where many parents fail is in their ability to raise emotionally stable children. On the other hand, physical, mental, sexual or spiritual abuse can cause us to become stagnant in our emotions. Feeling disconnected or alienated from one or both parents, or from siblings, can also cause emotional numbness.

We can also experience emotional numbness if we witness violence, get sexually assaulted or go through anything that we didn't have the capacity to handle emotionally and psychologically at the time. For this reason, emotional numbness is often one of the symptoms of conditions such as anxiety disorders and post-traumatic stress disorder (PTSD).

WHY IS EMOTIONAL NUMBNESS DANGEROUS?

Emotional numbness is often the root cause of many of life's problems because it leads to physical, mental, emotional and spiritual issues. These include somatic (caused by the mind) and chronic illness, addictions, fatigue, confusion, disconnection from the inner self, incapacity to form loving and close relationships or enjoy life, spiritual emptiness, depression, and dysfunctional coping mechanisms such as obsessive compulsive disorder (OCD). In very extreme cases, emotional numbness can lead a person to evil acts such as murder.

EMOTIONAL NUMBNESS – THE "SECRET ILLNESS"

Emotional numbness is referred to as the secret illness because it has become so socially acceptable that no one pays it any attention. In a society that doesn't know how to deal with strong emotions in a healthy way, refusing to acknowledge them is valued. The cool, calm and collected facade is respected, and it is this respect that strengthens our unhealthy detachment from our feelings. Emotional numbness is like a cancer that we don't know is there while it eats away at the body, but eventually, it comes to the surface.

SIGNS YOU ARE SUFFERING FROM EMOTIONAL NUMBNESS

When you are in full control of your emotions, emotional detachment can be a good thing. Emotional detachment helps you avoid becoming overwhelmed by other people's negative energy and it allows you to create boundaries. However, emotional detachment becomes the evil twin when it turns into emotional numbness, that automatic defense mechanism that wants to protect you from feeling difficult emotions. Here are some signs that you are suffering from emotional numbness:

- Emotional and physical flatness (you just feel dull)
- You don't feel complete, you know something is missing but can't figure out what

- People who express strong emotions, whether positive or negative, irritate you
- When strong emotions come to the surface, you panic
- You don't experience emotions in the mind, but you experience them in the body (for example: feeling sick when you are upset)
- You often withdraw from friends and family
- You feel distant from others
- You don't enjoy anything
- You live on autopilot
- Life doesn't feel real
- You can't express strong emotions

HOW TO BEAT EMOTIONAL NUMBNESS

There are several treatment options available to help you overcome emotional numbness. For some of you, the trauma might have been so severe that you've suppressed it. In cases like this, you will need to get your doctor to refer you to a therapist who will gently take you back to your childhood and assist you in uncovering the cause of your emotional numbness. A therapist will also provide you with better ways to cope with difficult emotions and experiences. Getting therapy will give you a safe space to approach, understand and express your emotions. The treatment options your therapist may offer you include:

Cognitive Behavioral Therapy (CBT): CBT will help you understand and express your emotions and evaluate the root cause of your emotional responses. CBT also examines the way you think and how you perceive the situations you experience because your thoughts and perceptions contribute to your emotions. The main aim of cognitive behavioral therapy is to transform your thought process so you no longer view yourself as powerless and vulnerable, but as strong and emotionally competent.

Acceptance and Commitment Therapy (ACT): Acceptance and commitment therapy is often used to treat conditions such as post-traumatic stress disorder, of which avoidance and emotional numbness is a symptom. Acceptance and commitment therapy uses mindfulness to get you to recognize the process you go through to suppress your emotions so that you can acknowledge your feelings and work through them. At the same time, ACT provides you with the tools you need to live a fulfilling life. In short, ACT helps you accept your feelings and commit to living a life that will benefit you and everyone else around you.

Mindfulness Strategies: For those of you who understand the root of your emotional numbness, you can start from here. Mindfulness is simply about slowing down and becoming more aware. We live in a very fast-paced environment, we celebrate multi-tasking, busyness, and being on the run, and believe that it makes us more productive. In her book *Make Your Brain Smarter,* Dr. Sandra Bond Chapman argues against this frantic pace, and instead advocates that single-tasking and slowing ourselves down drives much better results when it comes to productivity.

Mindfulness helps us focus inwardly, it teaches us to pay more attention to our body, mind, emotions and environment. Mindfulness allows us to be truly present in the moment we are in without holding back. We become who we were born to be because we learn to understand ourselves, appreciate ourselves and value ourselves. Mindfulness gives us more energy and better focus because our brains are no longer invested in fighting against our emotions. Here are some mindfulness exercises you can do every day to help you overcome emotional numbness:

Meditation: Meditation is the practice of being still. Contrary to popular belief, it isn't about emptying the mind and thinking about nothing. This misconception is often why people choose not to meditate because they try it once and realize how difficult it is to think about nothing. Meditation is about focusing on one thing and taking control of our thoughts. When we meditate, our identities are separated from our thoughts and this gives us the mental space we need to understand our thoughts and feelings, and release them. You don't need to be religious or a monk to meditate, nor do you need soothing background music and candles. You can meditate anywhere at any time.

There are several benefits associated with meditation. It helps us understand how we are feeling emotionally, and it helps us control our thoughts. When we are anxious or depressed, it is difficult to focus. It's easy to get lost in our thoughts and connect them to our identity; some meditation exercises involve categorizing thoughts by putting them into boxes, onto a conveyor belt or into balloons and allowing them to float off into the sky. Meditation helps us distance ourselves from our thoughts and remind us that they are not connected to our identity, and nor do they define our circumstances.

There is no best or worst time to meditate, so do it when it's most convenient for you. What's important is that you make time for meditation every day. Another misconception is that you need to meditate for extended periods of time, or you won't reap the benefits. You can mediate for as long or as short as you like; I started with two minutes per day because I couldn't concentrate for any longer than that. The aim is that you are properly focused while you are meditating or there is no point to it. Someone might meditate for an hour but keep losing focus, but someone else might meditate for two minutes with proper focus and reap more benefits. Here are the steps you will need to take to meditate:

- Set a timer for however long you can manage; it might be one, two or five minutes.
- Sit or lie down in a comfortable position (it is more common for people to sit).
- Decide which technique you are going to use.
- Close your eyes and take deep breaths.
- Focus on your breathing.
- Start imagining a favorite relaxing scene.
- If your thoughts start drifting from the scenery, bring them back by focusing on your breath.
- At the end of your session, bring your awareness back to the present moment, back to your body and back to the room.

After meditating I would advise writing in a journal to reflect on your experience. Did you find it difficult? Did your mind keep wandering? How did you feel afterwards? Also, you might want to try using different meditation techniques and see which one works best for you.

Incorporate meditation into your daily routine and will find that you get better at it over time. Also, the more you practice, the more you will start experiencing the benefits.

Breathing Exercises:

- Sit or stand in a comfortable position, inhale and exhale slowly while counting to six.
- Slowly inhale through your nose and exhale through your mouth allowing your breath to effortlessly flow in and out of your body.
- Surrender your thoughts, stop thinking about what you need to do get done, the dinner you need to cook, the bills you need to pay or any other worries you might have. When the thoughts come, don't dwell on them, let them float by like clouds.
- Pay attention to your breath, the way it enters your body and fills you with life and then leaves.

Mindful Awareness: The aim of this exercise is to increase your awareness of the daily tasks you typically perform without thinking about them, and being grateful for how completing them makes your life easier.

- Think of something that you do every day several times a day, such as opening a door.
- When you put your hand on the doorknob, take a moment to think about how you feel, where you are and what is on the other side of the door you are about to walk through.

Mindful awareness can also center around your thoughts. The majority of our thoughts are subconscious, but the moment you realize you are thinking a negative thought, stop and consider the thought. Label it as harmful and release it.

Or, anytime you are cooking, you can take a moment to appreciate how lucky you are to have food to eat and to share it with friends and family.

The aim of mindful awareness is that you don't go through your day on autopilot. You stop and think about your interactions and appreciate how blessed you are to be able to perform them, and how they enrich your life.

Mindful Immersion: The aim of this exercise is to learn how to be content in our present situation instead of feeling the constant pressure we put on ourselves to do better. Instead of rushing to complete one task so you can move onto the next, fully experience it and pay attention to the things that you wouldn't normally. For example, when you are cleaning the house, feel the motions while vacuuming the floor. When you are washing the dishes, pay attention to the muscles that are being used. When you are cleaning the windows, think of a way that you can clean them better, while making life easier on your wrists.

Mindful Appreciation: Mindful appreciation is about appreciating things in your day that you would never normally pay much attention to. For example, the postman who delivers your mail, the electricity that heats or lights your home, the eyes that allow you to see the sunrise every morning, or the mug that allows you to drink your coffee. Instead of just acknowledging these things or people, take it a step further and consider the following points:

- Do you know how any of these processes work?
- How do these things benefit your life and the lives of others?
- What would your life be like if you didn't have these things?

- Have you ever paid attention to the details?
- Have you ever stopped to think about how these things are connected and all play a role in the world?

To use mindful appreciation, choose five things that you know you will experience throughout your day. They can be people or objects. Write them down on a notepad, and as you come across each one, ask the above questions.

Mindful Listening: Most people are terrible listeners. Instead of paying attention to what another person is actually saying, our time is spent thinking about how to respond, or finishing their sentences. The next time you have a conversation with someone, make sure you are fully present. Listen to every last word, and to make sure you heard correctly, once they've finished speaking, repeat what they say. Think carefully about what the person has said before giving them an answer.

You can also practice mindful listening by listening to music without being influenced by past experiences or preconceptions. Most of the time, unless it's a song we haven't heard before, when we do hear a song we are familiar with, we either like it or dislike it, depending on how it made us feel. For example, if you listened to a certain song when you were breaking up with your partner, you are more inclined not to like it because of the emotions that resurface. Or you might have a disdain for heavy metal music because you think it glorifies a culture you don't agree with. The main aim of this exercise is to listen to music free from judgement.

- Choose a neutral song (or piece of instrumental music) you've never heard before.
- Don't pay any attention to the genre, the title of the song or the name of the artist.

- Play the song and flow with it until the end.
- Allow yourself to get lost in the beat, the instruments, the words and everything else that comes with the song.
- Pay attention to the tone of the singing voice, the different ranges; is there more than one voice?
- Don't think about the song, just hear it.

Mindful Observation: We live in a beautiful world, but rarely do we pay attention to it because of the busyness of life. Mindful observation is about focusing on nature and appreciating how awesome it truly is.

- Focus on an element of nature: it could be the sun, the moon, the sky, the flowers or the grass. Observe it for a couple of minutes.
- Don't think about it, just look until you lose focus. Look at it as if you've never seen it before.
- Observe every angle of it and become consumed by the presence of the object you are looking at.
- Submerge yourself in its energy and think about the role that it plays on the earth.

LIFESTYLE CHANGES

If you are seeing a therapist, they may also recommend lifestyle changes to assist you in overcoming emotional numbness. Stagnation, a bad diet, not getting enough sleep and isolating yourself can contribute to your condition. You may find that lifestyle changes are all you need to become unstuck.

Physical Exercise: Exercise is one of the most important lifestyle changes you can make. Several studies have concluded that physical activity helps to reduce the symptoms associated with conditions such as depression and anxiety because it stimulates the body and triggers the release of feel-good hormones such as endorphins and serotonin.

Depending on your level of fitness, walking is a great place to start. Research suggests that just 30 minutes of walking a day can greatly reduce the risk of chronic physical conditions as well as depression and anxiety.

Eat a Healthy Diet: The brain is in a constant state of activity and needs a constant supply of the right nutrients to function at its best. A poor diet can slow down the production of important neurotransmitters which will make it difficult to overcome emotional numbness. Here are a few tips on eating a healthy diet:

Plant-Based: The majority of calories in your diet should come from fruits, vegetables and whole-grain products. Plant-based foods are low in fat and provide plenty of minerals and vitamins needed to keep the body in good working order.

The United States Department of Health and Human Services (HHS) recommends adding all vegetable subgroups to your meals throughout the week. These include legumes such as beans and peas, and red, orange and dark green vegetables. Fruits, vegetables, cereals and whole-grain breads are high in fiber. Fiber helps reduce the risk of some cancers and heart disease, and it also keeps the bowels healthy. Half of your overall grain intake should include whole grains.

Calcium-Rich Foods: Get your calcium through fat-free or low-fat milk. If you don't consume dairy products, you can get it through other calcium-rich foods such as spinach, okra, curly kale, soya drinks, foods made with fortified flour, pilchards and sardines.

Reduce Trans and Saturated Fats: Trans and saturated fatty acids are the most dangerous type of fat because they raise blood cholesterol levels. If possible, eliminate them from your diet altogether, or eat a very limited amount. The fat from milk products and meat are the main sources of saturated fat in the majority of diets. Therefore, consume low-fat milk products, fish, poultry and lean meats. Health experts also recommend that you significantly reduce your intake of processed and red meats as this will assist in preventing chronic illness. A lot of ingredients in bakery products such as partially hydrogenated oils and palm oil also contain trans fatty acids and saturated fats. Additionally, it is advised that you cook with healthy oils such as olive or almond, instead of butter.

Reduce Salt and Sugar Intake: The majority of pre-packaged and processed foods are high in salt, sugar and other unhealthy additives. You can reduce your intake of these products significantly by cooking your food from scratch. Whole foods contain natural salts and sugars that are required for a healthy diet. However, even though salt and sugar are naturally occurring, it is still important to monitor your intake. Health experts advise that they should not amount to more than 10% of your daily calories. Studies suggest that a high salt/sodium intake is responsible for high blood pressure and some types of cardiovascular disease. Experts recommend that salt/sodium intake is kept below 2300 mg per day.

Portion Control: The food portions on food labels and in restaurants are a lot bigger than the recommended portions for effective weight management. It is even more important that you limit portion sizes of foods that are high in calories such as oils, fats, fried and baked goods. Here is a simple portion size guide you can use:

- *High-Fat Foods:* The size of one thumb for women; the size of two thumbs for men.
- *High-Carb Foods:* The size of one cupped hand for women; the size of two cupped hands for men.
- *Salads and Vegetables:* The size of one fist for women; the size of two fists for men.
- *High Protein Foods:* The size of one palm for women; the size of two palms for men.

Look After Your Gut: Eating fermented foods such as miso and yogurt, and taking probiotic supplements with a minimum of two live cultures, such as bifidobacterium and lactobacillus, will keep your digestive system in good working order.

Eliminate Drinks with Added Sugar: Studies have found that people who drink more than four cans of soda every day are four times more likely to suffer from depression than people who consume healthier drinks. Emotional numbness is one of the symptoms of depression.

Foods that Will Elevate Your Mood

As well as eating a standard healthy diet, there are a lot of healthy foods you can eat that will elevate your mood and give you plenty of energy to keep you refreshed throughout the day.

Lentils and Beans: Lentils and beans are plant-based proteins that are high in fiber and packed with feel-good nutrients. They are a powerful source of B vitamins which are good mood enhancers because they increase levels of neurotransmitters such as dopamine, serotonin, gamma aminobutyric (GAMA) and norepinephrine. All of these play an important role in mood regulation. Additionally, vitamin B plays an important role in nerve signaling. Nerve signaling is responsible for allowing nerve cells to communicate properly. When the body is deficient in vitamins such as folate and B12, it can cause depression. Additionally, beans and lentils are rich sources of non-heme iron, selenium, magnesium and zinc.

Seeds and Nuts: Raw nuts and seeds contain fiber, healthy fats and plant-based proteins. Additionally, they contain the amino acid tryptophan which is responsible for the production of the mood-enhancing hormone serotonin. Experts advise that you eat plenty of sunflower seeds, sesame seeds, pumpkin seeds, walnuts, peanuts, cashews and almonds. Furthermore, one study found that people who ate walnuts reduced their risk of becoming depressed by 23%. Finally, pine nuts, almonds and brazil nuts are good sources of selenium and zinc. These minerals are essential for the brain to operate at its full capacity. Research suggests that a deficiency in these minerals is linked to higher rates of depression.

Berries: A diet high in antioxidants reduces the inflammation that causes mood disorders such as depression. Berries are packed with phenolic compounds and antioxidants which are required for eliminating oxidative stress. Oxidative stress occurs when there is an imbalance between free radicals and antioxidants. Berries are also high in anthocyanins and this is what gives berries their bluish purple color. According to research, a diet high in anthocyanins reduces symptoms of depression by 39%.

Oats: Oats are a good source of fiber: one cup of raw oats contains 8 grams of fiber. When you eat a bowl of oats for breakfast, not only do you remain full until lunchtime, you also have plenty of energy. The reason for this is that fiber slows down the rate at which your system digests carbohydrates, which causes an incremental release of sugar into the bloodstream that keeps your energy levels stable. One study found that participants who ate 1.6-6 grams of fiber for breakfast had high energy levels and were in a better mood than those who didn't. When blood sugar levels are stable, it helps to control irritability and mood swings. Although whole grains in general are a good source of fiber, oats carry the advantage because they are also high in iron and provide 19% of your recommended daily intake. Anemia is one of the most common mineral deficiencies and it is caused by low iron. Its symptoms include mood disorders, sluggishness and fatigue.

Bananas: Bananas contain vitamin B6 which helps trigger the production of feel-good hormones such as serotonin and dopamine. One large banana contains 3.5 grams of fiber and 16 grams of sugar. When combined with fiber, sugar is gradually released into the bloodstream and this stabilizes blood sugar levels, giving you better control over your emotions. Low blood sugar causes mood swings and irritability. Additionally, when bananas are slightly green, they are a good source of prebiotics. Prebiotics is a type of fiber that plays a role in feeding healthy bacteria in the gut. A strong gut microbiome reduces the incidence of mood disorders.

Fermented Foods: Fermented foods such as sauerkraut, kombucha, kefir, yogurt and kimchi assist in improving mood and gut health. The fermentation process creates probiotics. These microorganisms help healthy bacteria grow in the gut, and research suggests that the healthy bacteria increase levels of serotonin. Please bear in mind that not all fermented foods contain probiotics. Wine, bread and beer are cooked and filtered and therefore do not produce probiotics during the fermentation process. Research suggests that there is a strong link between reduced rates of depression and healthy gut bacteria.

Dark Chocolate: What wonderful news! You can still eat chocolate and live a healthy lifestyle! Sugar contains a combination of feel-good ingredients such as N-acylethanolamine, theobromine and caffeine. It is also high in flavonoids which help to increase blood flow to the brain, improve brain health and reduce inflammation, all of which play an important role in mood regulation. Finally, the taste, texture and smell of dark chocolate are also responsible for the feel-good factor and help improve mood.

In case you are thinking, *"Well, I don't like dark chocolate, why can't I eat milk chocolate?"* Good question... that's because milk chocolate contains extra ingredients such as fat and sugar, which as you have read, are not good for you. It is also important to mention that you should eat dark chocolate in moderation, 1-2 small squares per day is enough.

Fatty Fish: Fatty fish is high in omega-3 fatty acids, and the only way to get them is through food because the body doesn't produce them. Fatty fish such as albacore tuna and salmon both contain types of omega-3 that are linked to low levels of depression. Omega-3 fatty acids keep the membrane for the brain cells flexible; they also play an important role in cell signaling and brain development.

Foods that Will Put You in a Bad Mood

There are so many foods that are bad for you, I could write an entire book on them! That's why I urge you to do your own research and educate yourself further about the foods you should stay away from. One of the main reasons why it's important to do some additional research is that, as you will find out from the following list, there are some foods that are marketed as being good for you, but they are not.

I am in no way suggesting that you shouldn't treat yourself every now and then, but whether you are suffering from emotional numbness or not, you should severely limit your intake of the following foods:

Cold Cuts: Packaged meats such as turkey, hot dogs, bologna and ham are high in nitrates, additives, artificial coloring and food preservatives. These chemicals are responsible for altering moods and draining energy. They also cause water retention, headaches and bloating. Nutritionist Adrian Boyer recommends roasting your own meat and slicing it to make your sandwiches. Not only is this method healthier, it's also a lot cheaper.

Salted Peanuts: Most people assume that peanuts are good for them; unfortunately, not all peanuts are created equally. Store-bought peanuts contain a chemical called MSG, an artificial flavoring that leaves you feeling moody, fatigued and weak, and also causes terrible headaches. Experts recommend that you purchase raw nuts, roast them and add some salt and herbs of your choice.

Processed, Packaged Seeds: Another form of dietary deception comes from processed, packaged seeds. Although they are very healthy when consumed raw or roasted at home, the processed kind are typically preserved using a chemical called potassium bromate. When treating people for depression, psychologists often examine thyroid levels as it is one of the main contributors to the condition, and overexposure to potassium bromate has been linked to thyroid issues. Processed and packaged seeds are also packed with dangerous food additives and sodium.

Dried Fruits: When most people see the word "fruit" they immediately assume it's healthy. Unfortunately, this is not always the case. Fruits are dried through a dehydration process which means they lose water. Since the fruits no longer contain water, two things happen. Firstly, water dilutes the natural sugars present in fruit; therefore, which means you are consuming too much sugar. Dried fruit also contains high levels of preservatives and additives. Second, water makes you feel full, and since there is no water in dried fruits, you are likely to overeat them. Although the fibre in the dried fruit acts as a buffer against a blood sugar spike, if you eat too much it can disturb the gut. Ideally, you should eat fresh fruit, but if you do eat dried fruit, control your portion sizes.

Potato Chips: The majority of potato chips are fried in vegetable oil. Vegetable oil is high in omega-6 fatty acids and saturated fats. Omega-6 fatty acids are the evil twin of omega-3 fatty acids and they work against the good that omega-3 does for the body. Omega-6 fatty acids are responsible for inflammation in the body, which can lead to mental and emotional instability.

Wheat: Once again, not all wheat is created equal. Some people will find that wheat puts them in a bad mood. One of the main reasons for this is that it contains gluten, which research suggests can cause mental fog and inflammation.

Cereals: The majority of store-bought cereals are high in refined carbohydrates and contain processed ingredients. Refined carbohydrates interfere with your blood sugar levels which causes mood swings. Several studies have concluded that extreme changes in blood sugar levels cause depression.

Coffee: Coffee is only bad for you if you drink too much of it. Coffee triggers the release of the main stress hormone cortisol. This causes a spike in energy levels and enables high mental and physical performance. However, when you crash, you feel exhausted and depleted of both physical and mental energy. Experts warn that those who drink more than four cups of coffee per day are at risk of chronic disorders such as anxiety, depression, mood swings and adrenal fatigue. Therefore, if you are going to drink coffee, limit it to 2 or 3 cups per day.

Processed Foods: The majority of processed foods are high in additives, preservatives, saturated fats and refined sugars. These chemicals disrupt our emotional and mental functions, causing us to feel unmotivated, uninspired, tired, anxious, exhausted and depressed.

Canned Foods: Again, because vegetables are healthy, people assume it is okay to eat them in any form. Canned foods are not only high in sodium, but they also contain a chemical additive called BPA which is linked to several chronic mood disorders such as anxiety and depression.

French Fries: French fries are full of salt, saturated fats and refined carbohydrates. These ingredients have a terrible effect on your mood; they give you a fake "high" that makes you feel energetic and alert. However, once you crash, you feel foggy, tired, irritable and sluggish.

Margarine: Margarine is another food that the average person assumes is good for them. But margarine is high in processed saturated fats which upset blood sugar levels. Continuous spikes in blood sugar cause rapid mood swings.

Baked Goods: Pies, cakes, muffins and cookies all contain high levels of saturated oils and refined sugars. These ingredients cause you to feel depressed, lethargic and heavy. They also send you on a constant emotional rollercoaster.

Vegetable Shortening: According to Boyer, vegetable shortening is high in omega-6 fatty acids and industrial fats. As we know, these have a negative effect on insulin levels and cancel out the positive effects of omega-3 fatty acids.

Agave Nectar: Agave nectar is loaded with fructose, and excess fructose is the cause of metabolic syndrome. Symptoms of this condition include mood instability and brain shrinkage. Again, agave nectar is one of the many foods promoted as a healthy alternative to sugar when the reality is that it is just as bad.

Bagels: Another food responsible for spiking blood sugar levels is bagels. These simple carbohydrates are made from white grains and they are devoid of any nutritional value. The blood sugar spike is made even worse if the bagel isn't eaten with a protein such as peanut butter.

Cocktail Mixers and Fruit Juices: Although it's fun to make your own cocktails at home, using store-bought mixers and fruit juices is a bad idea. They are very similar to soda drinks because they are loaded with sugar. The negative effects are also the same in that they give you a false and temporary energy boost. However, once you crash, you end up feeling depressed, irritable and fatigued.

Alcohol: Alcohol is a depressant; therefore, if you want to overcome emotional numbness, it is essential that you refrain from consuming alcohol.

Get Enough Sleep

Not getting enough sleep has a negative effect on how you feel. One of the reasons for this is that the neurotransmitters responsible for supporting our emotions are restored while we sleep. Therefore, we need to get the right amount of sleep in order for our brains to function at their full potential. People who don't get enough sleep increase their chances of suffering from depression and other mood-related disorders. Furthermore, research suggests that sleep deprivation contributes to negative thinking and anxiety. Experts recommend that adults get between seven to nine hours of sleep per night.

A Support Group

Having a good support group to help you through this season of your life will ensure your success. Not only will they cheer you on, but they will also act as accountability partners to ensure you are doing your part to overcome emotional numbness. Most of your friends and family members are probably not aware you are going through this, and you don't need to tell everyone. Speak to the people you know you can trust to be there for you when the going gets rough.

Stress Reduction

Too much stress makes us feel anxious, depressed and frustrated. These negative feelings make it difficult to challenge emotional numbness. Stress is a natural part of life and we can't avoid it, but we can minimize it. Here are a few tips:

- Identify the things/people in your life that are causing you stress. If having too many notifications on your phone causes you stress, turn them off. If you've got toxic friends, create boundaries and keep them at arm's length. If you have a bad habit of overspending, restructure your budget.
- Incorporate relaxation techniques such as meditation into your daily routine.
- Spend at least one day a week doing nothing so that you can recharge your batteries and prepare yourself for the week ahead.

Thoughts and Emotions

Feelings of hopelessness, helplessness and negative attitudes can upset the hormonal balance and deprive the brain of the chemicals required to experience positive emotions such as peace and happiness. Our thoughts and emotions can also affect our immune system and overall physical health. There are several things we can do to begin the process of protecting our thoughts and emotions, and these include:

Removing Yourself from Negative Situations: For example, if you are working in a job you hate and it makes you feel miserable and depressed, you might want to start looking for a job you know you will enjoy. Being in an unfulfilling relationship can also have a negative effect on your thoughts and emotions. It's not always that simple to walk out of a relationship, especially if you are married. But if you've tried everything to make things work and nothing's changing, leaving might be your only option if you are going to protect your peace.

Refocus: It's easy to think the worst when you are in a bad situation. You might be on your way to a meeting and there's loads of traffic. Typically, your immediate response is to get frustrated. But instead of focusing on the fact that you are stuck in traffic and might be late, practice gratitude. Say thank you that you are sitting in the comfort of your car. If it's a sunny day, focus on the weather. The aim is to shift your attention from the negative to something positive.

Change Your Perspective: It's easy to get stuck in the negative thinking trap when you choose to see things one way. Let's say you've just started a new job and the manager doesn't seem very friendly. Your first thought is that he/she doesn't like you. But the reality is that you are not a mind reader and you have no real evidence to substantiate your claims. So instead of making the assumption that your manager doesn't like you, attribute their behavior to their own stress.

Invest in Your Purpose

Most people struggle with their life's purpose. Since the beginning of time, man has asked, "Why was I put on the earth? After all, for the majority, life is very mundane; we work for 40 years just to pay bills and then we die. For some people, life can feel really pointless. Research has found that people who understand their purpose are a lot more resilient and are better able to handle life's disappointments. A strong sense of purpose provides a psychological buffer against challenges. Therefore, people who understand why they are here remain satisfied with life even when they are going through difficult situations.

If you are not sure what your purpose is, start thinking about it. What are you naturally gifted at? What brings you joy? What do people closest to you say you are good at? If you can answer these questions, you are one step closer to your purpose. When you find out what it is, start investing in it. If dancing is your gift, join a dance class; if writing is your gift, take a writing course; if speaking is your gift, take a public speaking course. Whatever your gift is, perfect it so that when the opportunity arises, you are ready to take it.

There is a lot more to negative emotions than what you feel in the moment and the emotions you are aware of. As mentioned, some of them are so deeply buried you don't know they exist, but because emotions are powerful energy forces, they are silently working against you. In Chapter 5, you will learn all about trapped emotions and how you can overcome them.

CHAPTER 5

TRAPPED EMOTIONS – THE NEGATIVE EMOTIONS YOU ARE UNAWARE OF

Trapped emotions are extremely dangerous because we don't know we are carrying them. Some events in life are so traumatic that the only way the brain can cope is by repressing them. Even if your conscious mind doesn't remember the event, the subconscious mind does, and it is this stored information that controls the inner workings of the body.

TRAPPED EMOTIONS – WHAT ARE THEY?

The body is not designed to hold on to emotions. They are supposed to flow through the body. When we experience the emotion of sadness and cry, we feel better; when we laugh, we feel good. When you slice your finger while chopping onions, it feels slightly better when you scream out in pain. When you are frustrated with a friend or a romantic partner, expressing your emotions makes you feel better. But an emotion gets trapped when you do not deal with the emotions that that came with a traumatic event and so you get stuck in that moment and are unable to move past the depression, grief, fear or anger. The negative emotional energy accumulated during that time remains in your body, which eventually causes physical, mental and emotional damage.

Coleen's Resentment: Coleen was one of three children raised by an emotionally abusive mother. But for some reason, her other two siblings did not experience the same abuse. Coleen felt as if her mother had a unique hatred for her alone so she couldn't wait to leave the family home and go to college. She graduated from one of the top universities in the country and went on to become a medical sales rep. From the outside, it looked as though Coleen had the perfect life, but at the age of 21, she was struck down with endometriosis, a crippling condition that attacks the womb. She spent weeks off work, and eventually her company was forced to terminate her employment, which was another emotional blow for Coleen. The doctors couldn't tell her the cause of her condition and nor could they cure it. They just kept giving her medication, she kept going into the hospital, but she wasn't getting any better.

Coleen's healing journey started with a hypnotist, but this hypnotist just so happened to also be an energy healer. Before a hypnosis session, the therapist will ask questions about family history, and it was at this point that Coleen's therapist began to suspect that her condition was connected to trapped emotions due to childhood trauma. This was all confirmed during the hypnosis session and the next stage involved energy healing. All her negative emotional blockages were released, and shortly after she was completely cured of endometriosis.

YOUR FUTURE HIJACKED

Do you ever feel like you just can't catch a break? You know that you are not living the life you desire to have. Your relationships are not satisfying, your career is crippling but any time you try and make improvements, you just can't seem to build momentum. You might even suspect that your past has something to do with your inability to move forward with the things that you desire.

In the Western world, the traditional psychological approach to confronting your past is to talk about it with a therapist and find the best coping mechanisms. In many cases, this works, however, there not much is known about trapped emotions, and as a result, many people never fully heal. Trapped emotions lead people to self-medicate in different ways; it can cause people to deflect by trying to resolve everyone else's problems, to use drugs and alcohol, or to become workaholics or risk takers. People are unable to fulfil their true potential, and they are constantly battling with themselves to make their life work the way they dream about. The majority of the time, the underlying cause of the frustration is a trapped emotion related to a traumatic event.

TRAPPED EMOTIONS ARE DESTRUCTIVE

Trapped emotions can cause you to sabotage your relationships, make the wrong assumptions, fly off the handle at an innocent remark, and misinterpret behavior. Additionally, trapped emotions can cause anxiety, depression and a host of other unwanted feelings that you can't seem to overcome no matter how much therapy you have. Additionally, they can cause physical ailments and destroy the body. Because these invisible emotions are never detected, doctors will keep prescribing medication to mask the symptoms, but the underlying cause has never been addressed, which is why full healing never manifests.

There are many reasons why people get sick, and trapped emotions is definitely one of them. Because they distort the body's energy field and they are invisible, they can cause severe damage. Trapped emotions destroy the immune system, prevent the normal function of glands and organs, block the flow of energy and distort body tissue. Here is a list of some diseases and conditions that may be caused by trapped emotions:

- Depression
- Lupus
- Vertigo
- Migraines
- Weight issues
- Joint pain
- Colitis
- Crohn's disease
- Chest pain
- Social anxiety

You have probably heard the saying, *"Time heals all wounds."* Unfortunately, this is not the case for invisible wounds.

How do I Heal From Trapped Emotions?

By now, you might be wondering whether you've got any trapped emotions. Or you may be thinking that you couldn't possibly have any trapped emotions because you've never experienced any traumatic events. Well, the reality is that everyone has been through a traumatic event in their life whether it felt like one or not. Here are a few examples:

- Rejection
- Physical, sexual, mental or verbal abuse

- Physical trauma
- Emotional or physical combat
- You or a loved one getting sick
- Abandonment or neglect
- Negative self-talk
- Negative feelings about yourself or others
- Abortion or miscarriage
- The death of a loved one
- Long-term stress
- Internalizing feelings
- Financial difficulty
- Feelings of inferiority
- Relationship problems or divorce

This list is basic, but there are thousands of incidents that count as trauma. You can find out whether you have trapped emotions by communicating with your subconscious mind. But first, let me give you an overview of the subconscious mind.

What is the Subconscious Mind?

The mind is made up of two parts, the conscious and the subconscious. The conscious mind is what we use to plan, make decisions, think, see, touch, taste, hear and perform all the other bodily activities that we are consciously aware of. However, the conscious part of the brain constitutes a very small portion of the mind. The majority of the brain plays a much more important role in who we are and the way our lives play out.

The subconscious mind is where everything we have seen, heard and experienced since we were in the womb is stored. Basically, as soon as you became a living being, your brain started recording everything it was exposed to. Think about it like the hard drive of a computer. It appears as if the keyboard and the screen is where all the action takes place, but that is a tiny fraction of the workings of a computer. Everything is stored on the hard drive; whatever you delete from your computer is never permanently deleted, it is stored on the hard drive and a professional will know how to retrieve it. Likewise, even though you can't remember things that happened during your childhood, your subconscious mind has access to that information because that is where it is stored. According to experts, by the age of 18, there is the equivalent of over 100 Britannica encyclopedias worth of information stored in the subconscious mind!

The subconscious mind doesn't just store information, it ensures our bodies function the way they are supposed to. It is also the driving force behind our behavior and our emotions. In the same way we give no consideration to the hard drive until something goes wrong with the computer, we pay no attention to the subconscious mind when in fact, it should be the part of the mind that we nurture the most. One interesting fact about the brain is that it has no pain-sensing nerves and so brain surgery is often performed when patients are awake so that doctors can get feedback from them. Dr. Wilder Penfield found that some people were able to remember events they had buried during brain surgery when certain areas of the brain were stimulated. These events were not remembered under normal circumstances, but when that area of the brain was touched again, the memory would resurface.

The subconscious mind holds every piece of information about your life including your trapped emotions and how they are affecting your mental, emotional and physical wellbeing. Your subconscious mind also knows what your body needs to heal itself. The question is, how do we access this information? According to Dr. George Goodheart, muscle testing is the answer. Dr. Goodheart discovered that muscle testing could be used to tap into the subconscious mind and access information required for healing.

HAVING A CONVERSATION WITH YOUR BODY

The human body is no different from other living organisms. For example, plants need light to survive; therefore, they will grow away from darkness and towards sunlight. The fish in the sea swim towards the light and away from the dark, which is how fishermen bait them and catch them for food. On a subconscious level, the human body operates in the same way. The body is drawn towards the positive and moves away from the negative. If you are ready to allow your subconscious mind to speak to your body, keep reading.

The Sway Test

The sway test is a simple method that will help you retrieve information from your subconscious mind about your emotional state. Here are the steps you will need to follow:

- Make sure you are in a quiet location with no distractions. Turn off the TV, radio and anything else that emits sound waves.
- Stand in a comfortable position with your feet shoulder width apart and your hands by your sides.
- Close your eyes and completely relax your body.

You will soon realize that it is impossible not to move your body because your muscles are always working to maintain your posture. So your body will start to move in different directions, these movements are very slight and you are not making them consciously. When you make a statement that is true, positive or congruent, within less than 10 seconds, your body will sway forwards slightly. When you make an untrue, negative, or incongruent statement, within ten seconds, your body will sway backwards slightly.

At this point, make the positive statement, "unconditional love." Once you've said it, think about the statement and connect with the emotions associated with it. Your body will sway forwards to indicate its agreement with the energy of this positive statement.

Stop thinking about unconditional love and say the word "war." Think about this word and connect with the negative emotions associated with it. Within ten seconds, you will sway backwards as your body attempts to move away from the negative energy associated with the word.

Now make a statement that you know to be explicitly true to you such as, *"My name is _____."* Your subconscious mind knows what is true and what is false; you will feel your body sway forward to a true statement and backward to a false statement.

Now make a statement that is untrue to you. For example, if your name is Joanna, say, *"My name is Linda."* Your subconscious mind will know that this statement is not true and your body will sway backwards.

It might take a bit of practice before your body reacts accordingly; however, the more you practice, the easier it will become. Once you are confident that the communication channels between your body and your subconscious mind have been opened, the next step is to determine whether you have any trapped emotions. You can do this by asking, *"Do I have any trapped emotions?"* If the answer is 'yes,' you will feel your body sway forwards, if the answer is 'no,' you will feel your body sway backwards.

MUSCLE TESTING

Now that you know you've got trapped emotions, the next step is to find out exactly what they are, and this is accomplished through muscle testing. There are several muscle tests you can try, all with varying degrees of difficulty. However, for the purposes of this book, I am highlighting the two that I have found to be the most effective.

The Elbow Test: The goal with the elbow test is to notice that there is a difference in resistance when something is true or false.

- Stand or sit with your arms by your side.
- Lift one arm so that it bends at the elbow and remains parallel to the floor.
- Your palm can face upwards or downwards.
- Do not relax your arm, it should be slightly stiff.
- With your opposite arm, use two fingers and position them next to the wrist bone of your bent arm.
- Say the word, "Yes," and push down slightly with your fingers.
- You will notice that your arm is difficult to push down.
- Say the word "No," and push down with your fingers.
- You will notice that your arm gives way slightly, and you are able to push your arm down with your two fingers.

Ring in Ring: The purpose of this muscle test is no different to the elbow or the sway test, namely, to discover whether a statement is true or false.

- Sit or stand in a comfortable position and make a circle with your middle finger and thumb.

- Make a circle with the middle finger and thumb of your other hand and link both circles together like a link on a chain.
- One hand will be the pressure ring and the other hand the resistance ring.
- When the answer is "yes," the resistance ring remains locked.
- When the answer is "no," the pressure ring will break.

THINGS THAT WILL AFFECT MUSCLE TESTING ACCURACY

There are several things that will affect the accuracy of your muscle test, these include the following:

- **Doubt:** If you have convinced yourself that it isn't going to work, then your mind isn't going to be open enough to get positive results. Belief that it is possible to eliminate trapped emotions is the first step to overcoming them.
- **Overload:** It is possible to have over 100 trapped emotions. In such a case, it will be too difficult to tune in. If you keep getting stuck, it is advised that you contact an expert to assist you in releasing trapped emotions.
- **Trying Too Hard:** The subconscious mind doesn't respond well to pressure. Trying too hard will create blockages and prevent you from tapping in. Relax and don't get frustrated when it doesn't work the first time around.

GETTING SPECIFIC ABOUT TRAPPED EMOTIONS

This chart is taken from the book *The Emotion Code* by Dr. Bradley Nelson. The emotion code chart will help you determine which trapped emotions you need to release. At first glance, it looks pretty complicated, but once you have a better understanding, you will find it easier to navigate.

	A	B
1 Small intestine or heart	Love unreceived Lost Forlorn Betrayal Abandonment	Vulnerability Insecurity Heartache Effort unreceived
2 Stomach or Spleen	Worry Nervousness Disgust Despair Anxiety	Low-self esteem Lack of control Hopelessness Helplessness Failure
3 Colon or lung	Sorrow Sadness Rejection Discouragement Crying	Stubbornness Self-abuse Grief Defensiveness Confusion
4 Gall bladder or liver	Resentment Hatred Guilt Bitterness Anger	Taken for granted Panic Indecisiveness Frustration Depression
5 Bladder or kidneys	Peeved Horror Fear Dread Blaming	Wishy-washy Unsupported Terror Creative insecurity Conflict
6 Sexual organs or glands	Overwhelm Lust Longing Jealousy Humiliation	Worthlessness Unworthiness Shock Shame Pride

Use the muscle test that's easiest for you and find the trapped emotions through a process of elimination. Start by asking yourself whether the trapped emotion is in column A, and you will get a yes or no answer. If the answer is "no," ask yourself whether the trapped emotion is in column B. If the answer is "Yes," you can move onto the next step.

There are six rows in each column, so your next step is to determine which row/rows the emotion is in. The most efficient way to do this is to ask yourself whether the emotion is in an odd or even row. If the emotion is in an odd row, go through the odd numbers 1, 3 and 5 and ask whether the trapped emotion is in any of those rows. If you discover that the trapped emotion is in column A row 1, you will have narrowed the emotions down to: Love unreceived, lost, forlorn, betrayal and abandonment. You can then go through each of these emotions one by one to determine which emotion/emotions are trapped.

HOW TO RELEASE TRAPPED EMOTIONS

Now that you know which emotions are trapped in the body, it's time to release them. It is important to mention that when it comes to releasing trapped emotions, you need to remember how the emotion came about. In some instances, the trauma may have been so difficult that you have completely repressed it. If this is the case, you will need to seek professional help to get at the root of your problem. Otherwise, here is a seven-step meditation exercise created by author and alternative medicine advocate Deepak Chopra.

STEP 1: IDENTIFY THE EVENT

Find some alone time completely free from distraction. Sit somewhere that is comfortable, yet sturdy like a meditation cushion or a blanket. Close your eyes and relax into the seated position.

Spend a few minutes focusing on your breath and then bring to mind an upsetting circumstance that caused the emotions you identified during the muscle test. Think about that incident in detail. How did it happen? Where did it happen? Who was involved? Think about the event as if you were a witness to it and now you are reporting it to a newspaper or to the police.

As you are watching the event, identify what you are feeling. Do you feel insulted, unappreciated or disgusted? Once you have labelled the feeling, focus on that word.

STEP 2: WITNESS THE EXPERIENCE

Slowly take your attention away from the word and allow it to settle on your body. Focus on the physical sensations that you experience in your body because of the emotion you've identified.

As you think about this experience, allow your attention to move throughout your body. As your memory brings up different sensations, pay attention to where they are taking place in your body. You might experience a tight sensation in the gut, or pressure in the throat or chest. Wherever you locate this experience in the body is where the emotion has been trapped.

STEP 3: EXPRESS HOW YOU FEEL

Express how you feel by putting your hand over the part of your body where the sensation is located. Say out loud, *"I can feel pain here."* If you have identified more than one location for the sensation, move to the other areas and repeat.

Physical discomfort is an indication that there is an imbalance in your spiritual, mental or physical experience. Every cell in your body is aware of this and it is important to embrace the wisdom that comes from these sensations because that is how you will heal.

STEP 4: TAKE RESPONSIBILITY

Regardless of the traumatic event that led to these feelings, the emotions belong to you and only you can get rid of them. No matter what a person has done to you, holding on to bitterness and anger is only damaging to you. Now that you have located these feelings, how you respond to the emotional turbulence is up to you. It is important that you refrain from feeling guilty about your emotions; you didn't cause them, and they are not your fault. Identifying your emotions means that you recognize that you have the ability to respond to your emotions in creative and new ways. When you take responsibility for your feelings, it empowers you to deal with those emotions in a way that will benefit you. You are no longer blaming people for what they did to you or blaming people for how your life has turned out; you have taken authority over those emotions, and you will now use them to your advantage.

STEP 5: RELEASE THE EMOTION

Focus your attention on the part of the body that's holding the pain, and as you breathe out, set your intention to release the pain. Do this continuously until you feel the pain leave your body. Some people find that it helps to make some type of noise such as humming while releasing the emotion as it assists in loosening the contraction.

STEP 6: SHARE THE OUTCOME

Speak to a trusted friend or family member about your experience, let them know how you went about releasing the negative emotions that were trapped in your body, and discuss the freedom you now feel that these emotions are no longer holding you hostage.

If the traumatic event involved another person, you can write that person a letter expressing that you have forgiven them for what took place. You can also thank them because the experience led to you becoming a stronger person. Explain that you have taken back your power and you can now share your pain without blaming or feeling emotional discomfort.

STEP 7: CELEBRATE YOUR SUCCESS

Releasing negative emotions is no easy process. The fact that you were even able to recognize that something was holding you back from living a fulfilling life is admirable. In order to enter into new dimensions and new realms of living, you must get comfortable with being uncomfortable. For many people, this is very difficult to achieve because most people become comfortable with their pain and their circumstances. This is especially true for those who are aware of the traumatic events they experienced because they tend to use it as an excuse for not doing more with their lives.

To celebrate, do something nice for yourself; book a vacation, go out to dinner or go shopping. Whatever you deem as a celebration, do it.

This is not a one-time exercise, so you may need to perform it several times to get some relief. The key is not to give up. I can tell you with confidence that it works, but it's up to you to make it work for you.

After reading the last few chapters, you may feel slightly dejected about the effect that negative emotions can have on you, right? That's understandable because there's nothing fun about low self-esteem, co-dependency and all the other consequences mentioned in these chapters. But the battle is not lost, because negative emotions can also be your most powerful asset if you know how to use them in the right way.

CHAPTER 6

THE POWER OF NEGATIVE EMOTIONS

With players like Magic Johnson, Byron Scott and Bob McAdoo, the Los Angeles Lakers were one of the best teams in the history of the game of basketball. But they had one major problem: they were inconsistent. When they were good, they were very good; on the other hand, when they were bad, they were very bad. So bad in fact that they did not even play in the 1986 NBA championships. Their main problem was a lack of focus. As the greatest team in history, they had lost their motivation. During the first half of one game, they were telling each other jokes, checking out the cheerleaders and paying zero attention to what was taking place on the court. At that time, Kareem Abdul-Jabbar was the star player, and he was the only one taking the game seriously. The coach Pat Riley sat quietly, observing this situation, and devised a plan to shake the players into action.

During half time, Riley packed them into the locker room, screamed at them and threw a tray full of cups of water in their direction. The only person who ended up drenched was the star player, the one everyone knew had his head in the game and didn't deserve the wrath of Riley. What they didn't know was that this was intentional; he wanted them to feel guilty so they would get it together – and that's exactly what happened.

Riley's strategy would have failed if he had gone into the locker room with a cool, calm attitude creating a loving and joyful atmosphere. The team members needed a dose of anger to trigger a positive reaction. In this case, it served as motivation and they went back onto the court and won the game, despite the fact that they were twenty points behind at half time. Sometimes it's necessary to embrace negative emotions. Society teaches us to look for the positive in everything, but by concealing, or hiding negative emotions, you will miss out on the benefits of those emotions.

In some cases, negative emotions also seem to get us the most favorable outcomes. Think back to a time when you had to deal with a customer service situation. For example, you received an email that your doctor's appointment had been changed to a date that was not convenient for you. The airline booked you the wrong flight, or your credit card company applied a late payment fee despite the fact that you couldn't make the payment because their system was down. When you get on the phone, what tone do you adopt? Nice and friendly, or to-the-point and assertive? Most people adopt the nice and friendly approach; but what do you find? It doesn't work. Why? Because the person on the other end of the phone has been trained to get the most favorable outcome for the company. It's only when they come across someone who knows their rights and isn't going to take "no" for an answer that they budge. The only way to get this tone across over the phone is to be assertive. In general, people don't like taking on such characteristics because of the negative connotations attached to them. But everyone likes having that one feisty friend who isn't afraid to say what they think; that friend who will kick up a fuss and get everyone an entire free meal because of one burnt French fry! No one wants to be that feisty one because they are labelled as having an "attitude" or worse, but we will gladly accept the benefits of having assertive friends.

Negative emotions also improve your focus. When you've got to bang a nail into a wall, that fear of hitting your finger instead of the nail intensifies your focus to ensure that you don't get hurt. Kate Harkness from Queen's University conducted a study that found people who are generally in a depressed mood notice more details. During the study, participants were asked to evaluate facial expressions. The cheerful group noticed the basics: eyes, nose, maybe a raised eyebrow. But the depressed people noticed things like the narrowing of the eyes, a lip quiver or a turned-up nose. For those of you in a relationship, what happens when you are having an argument with your partner? You pay close attention to them and notice the slightest change in body language. *"Don't roll your shoulders at me!" "Don't glare at me like that!" "Or don't give me that look of disgust!"* Sound familiar?

Air Traffic Control is an industry responsible for safety; therefore, the culture is generally one that is high in negative emotions because mistakes can lead to hundreds of deaths and millions of dollars lost. Employees must have a keen eye for detail. The majority of their day is spent looking at a screen with tiny little dots on it that represent airplanes and they each have their own flight plan, speed, altitude and call number. Negative emotions such as suspicion and anxiety act as beacons that draw attention to details that a mind operating at its normal capacity would miss. Air traffic controllers are not trained to focus on the things that go right; they are trained to focus on the things that go wrong. Planes that come within a three-mile radius of one another are in danger. The busiest time for an air traffic controller is during the night when Federal Express planes are flying. Boris is an air traffic controller in Atlanta, Georgia, and he says that his colleagues take great pride in their jobs, but they also have negative attitudes in general and they deal with it by joking with each other when they can, or by going home and drinking, or praying, depending on their beliefs.

Most people don't fully understand negative emotions and there appears to be a separation between the feeling itself, and the expression of negative feelings. Everyone will agree that it is normal to feel bad sometimes because life happens. But it is not uncommon for other people to feel irritated when they witness those emotions expressed intensely. Think about the last time you saw a couple arguing in the street, or someone angrily kicking a garbage can. Or a disagreement that got a bit loud in a store when a customer was given the wrong change. Everyone starts looking in disgust, no one is concerned about the person showing the emotion. The thought process of the onlookers is that he/she shouldn't be acting like this in public. However, what we don't consider is that expressing negative emotions is an important part of the human experience. If it wasn't for the frown and the downturned mouth, how would you know when the colleague you are about to approach to tell a joke isn't in the mood? When in a public space and someone gasps in horror, the adrenaline levels of those in the area increase and they look around to make sure they are safe.

WHY ARE WE SO AGAINST NEGATIVE EMOTIONS?

Would you like to repeat the public speaking nightmare you experienced when the group spent the whole time yawning and frowning instead of laughing when you told a joke? On the flip side, how many of you would like to relive the joy and excitement you experienced when your first child was born? Or wouldn't you just love to go back to that sun-soaked vacation in the Maldives you enjoyed last year? University professor Dr. Hi Po Bobo Lau conducted a study in which he asked participants to put a price tag on recreating the negative and positive experiences they have had in life. The results found that people would pay more to avoid pain. There was a high price attached to avoiding negative emotions. But the one emotion people desired to recreate the most was love. That's because as social creatures, we want to feel accepted, valued and cared for. However, despite the fact that the desire to be loved is normal, not everyone is going to love us. We can't control how people are going to receive us; when we walk into a room and meet a group of new people, some of them are going to like us, others are not. In some cases, no one will like you. We have no control over how other people perceive us, but we have full control over how we think and act. The feeling of uncertainty is a very uncomfortable psychological state. Additionally, the study found that the highest prices were also assigned to embarrassment and regret. In other words, the most valuable emotional states are all dependent upon other people's perceptions of us.

Psychologists suggest that there are four basic reasons why humans avoid negative emotions:

- They don't feel good.
- They represent feelings of stagnation.
- They represent a loss of control.
- They come with a negative social cost.

So, lets dig a little deeper here.

They Don't Feel Good: First, we avoid feeling bad because no one wants to feel bad. In other words, negative emotions are not pleasant. Who wants to spend the afternoon in a state of depression and anxiety? No one, right? However, the mistake that people make is not that they want to avoid the negative emotion, but rather that they underestimate their capacity to deal with these negative emotions. Each one of you reading this has experienced fear and anger at some point in your life. You didn't remain in that state, those feelings came and went and here you are today reading this book. In other words, they are not going to kill you. Not only do we avoid negative emotions because they don't feel good, we also avoid them because we don't think we can handle them.

Think about the last time you were bored in a social setting. According to psychologist Peter Toohey, boredom is a trigger alerting you to the fact that these interactions are not satisfying you. In some instances, there is nothing you can do about your boredom, such as when listening to a speech at work, or sitting on a plane with no reading material and you are not interested in the movies available. In others, you can leave and look for something more entertaining. Boredom acts as a functional tool. It is either a sign that you are not making the right choices such as when, for example, you are surrounding yourself with people that provide you with no mental stimulation. Or you are too judgemental; for example, every time you enter a new social environment, you make assumptions about the type of people that are there and as a result, avoid proper interactions. The point is that even though you hate being bored, you manage perfectly well when you are. Depending on your age, you have probably experienced boredom hundreds, if not thousands of times, and despite the discomfort, you've probably never focused on the fact that you handled it pretty well.

They Represent Feelings of Stagnation: Who wants to feel as if they are stuck and can't move? That feeling of hopelessness and despair that is never going to go away. It makes sense that no one wants to feel this way, and that is how emotions such as depression are perceived. But the reality is that the majority of people who experience depression do so in bouts. Please bear in mind, I am not referring to clinical depression here, but depressive episodes that people go through when something distressing happens in their life. Depressive episodes are referred to as 'episodes' because they don't last. So the fear that feelings such as anxiety and anger will have you trapped in an emotional prison that you will never escape is an irrational one, and you know this to be true from your own personal experience.

They Represent a Loss of Control: Another reason why we avoid negative emotions is we believe they will take full control over us and that we will no longer have restraint over what we do and say. Anger is the most obvious culprit for this fear; there is a slight element of truth to this as there have been several cases where severe bodily harm, and even murder have resulted during a fit of rage and the person regretted their actions shortly after committing the act. Lashing out in anger is one of the reasons why second- degree murder exists in the United States justice system. It's an acknowledgement that even though a life was taken, the perpetrator didn't plan it, but instead, became a victim of their own anger. Nevertheless, it is extremely rare for people to lash out in this way and take someone's life because they were unable to control their temper.

It is highly unlikely that your fit of rage will get you a slot on cable TV news. But it can affect us in some unconventional ways. Have you ever wondered where the term 'hot-headed' came from? Well, a group of researchers were interested in whether there was any truth associated with the term. They conducted a study where some participants were presented with words related to anger such as irritated, hostile, and scornful. They were told that the words were related to a memory experiment. In another task, the same participants were asked whether the temperatures of cities they had no knowledge of were on average hot or cold. The researchers found that the group who were exposed to the angry words were more likely to state that the towns were hot.

They Come with a Negative Social Cost: We also avoid negative emotions because we don't want to deal with the social consequences associated with expressing them. We come to these conclusions through social observations. Everyone avoids the negative Nigels in the office, that one employee who never has anything good to say. Or the uncle we avoid because they fly off the handle unjustifiably. There is some truth to the social costs associated with expressing negative emotions, but they are not as serious as we have been conditioned to believe.

On the other hand, our moods can affect others. Psychologist Thomas Joiner evaluated the affect that negative emotions had on roommates. He discovered that when one person was depressed, someone else would experience depression shortly afterward. His findings were true even in the absence of distressing life events. In other words, a depressive state of mind is contagious regardless of the circumstances. Additionally, Joiner found that it was easier for a depressed roommate to affect happy roommates than it was for a happy roommate to affect a depressed roommate. Thomas Joiner concluded that negative emotions are more powerful than positive emotions.

Now that I have gone through all the reasons why people avoid negative emotions, it should be clear that these reasons are valid. As we know, negative emotions exist, but the question is: why? What purpose do they serve? Negative emotions are healthy when they are channelled in the right direction. Although they are unpleasant, difficult, and problematic at times, they do have their advantages. Our emotions are our own personal communication network, they inform us of our progress. When we feel good, we know we are headed in the right direction, when we feel bad, we know something needs to change. Avoiding your emotions is possibly one of the most psychologically damaging things you can do. Let me ease you into this a little bit:

- You want to feel fear when you are in a dangerous situation and there is a possibility that you could get harmed.
- You want to feel that jolt of anger when you need to defend your younger sibling.
- You want to feel frustration when you keep failing your driving test.
- You want to feel regret when you say something mean and nasty to someone in the heat of the moment.

In the above examples, these emotions are alerting you to the fact that something is wrong and your attention is required. Trying to suppress the anger or any other negative emotion does not give you insight about why you are feeling this way and what you need to do about the situation. If you are finding it difficult to understand why negative emotions are important, think about it like this. Imagine living in a world where no one felt fear when a stranger was following them in the street.

Just think how many people have escaped death because their instincts told them to run when they felt they were in danger. Or imagine a world where people weren't moved by anger when someone was falsely accused of a crime and sentenced to life in prison. Without these emotions, human beings would not function properly. In the following sections we will evaluate some of the most unpopular negative emotions.

THE BENEFITS OF ANGER

Anger has a justifiably bad reputation; it is the cause of many of the problems we have in the world today such as violence, hatred and war. On the surface, you could argue that the world would be a better place without anger. However, many mental health professionals, brain scientists, and social and evolutionary psychologists believe that there are several advantages to anger, and when channelled in the right direction, it can improve the human condition. When emotions are analyzed from an evolutionary perspective, to some degree, all emotions are useful, and that includes anger.

Justin is a champion MMA fighter, he is very well known in his field, but if you are not into the sport, you won't know who he is. During a vacation in Mexico, he stops off at a street vendor to buy some local food. As the young woman hands him his container, a very tall and muscular man walks over and starts screaming at the woman to serve him a plate. It's a tourist location so there are plenty of people around, but no one is big enough or brave enough to confront the guy. He continues shouting at the woman who appears visibly shaken and afraid. As a trained fighter, Justin begins paying attention to his surroundings and notices that everyone is getting nervous. As the guy continues shouting, Justin calmly turns to face the man and says, "Excuse me, I would really appreciate it if you would lower your voice." The man looks at Justin for a couple of seconds and then continues screaming at the woman to fix him some food. Justin turns his voice up a notch and says, "Listen mate, there really isn't any need for you to be making such a scene, the lady isn't comfortable with the way you are speaking to her so can you leave." The big guy takes his attention off the woman and turns it onto Justin. He starts walking in his direction cursing at him. Justin walks towards him too and says, "In my town, this means you are looking for a fight, are you ready?" Despite the fact that Justin is shorter and smaller in build than him (you can compare it to a David and Goliath situation), Justin's boldness makes the man feel uncomfortable, and after sizing him up for a couple of seconds, he turns around and walks off.

Justin picks up his food and looks around expecting the bystanders and especially the woman he was defending to say thank you, nod, or do something to show their appreciation. Instead, they all act as if they are just as afraid of him as they were of the aggressor. In this instance, anger was an appropriate response from Justin, he was defending a woman who was unable to defend herself, and if Justin wasn't there, things could have ended very badly. But it still elicited a negative response from the bystanders. Like every other negative emotion, anger is only negative when it is used in the wrong way. According to experts, only ten percent of angry outbursts result in violence. The emotion of anger is stimulated when we feel we have been wronged in some way, or when something or someone is preventing us from getting what we want. In general, anger is caused by what another person did, didn't do, or might do. There are many benefits associated with anger; studies suggest that it boosts performance, creativity and optimism. Additionally, expressing anger motivates people to initiate change, and leads to more successful negotiations.

One study found that the group of people who had been induced to experience anger took more risks than the group who had not. Anger encouraged them to push the boundaries, so they were no longer content remaining in their comfort zone. Other studies have found that anger makes people feel as if they have more control over an outcome, and that the risks they took will pay off. Experts argue that since anger is an emotion that helps us handle threats, it is also helpful for preparing us to take action. This theory might explain why athletes psyche themselves up before competing by getting angry. Studies have also found that anger boosts creativity and angry people are more likely to perform better.

Anger also improves performance and encourages people to take action. When I was a teenager, my sisters and I took it in turns to wash the dishes during the week. I hated it, and when it was my turn, I would avoid it for as long as possible. The only thing that spurred me into action was hearing my dad's bellowing voice shouting from the bottom of the stairs to come and wash the dishes. I would jump off my bed so fast and wash those dishes until they were sparkling. Researchers studied a group of construction managers in England, and it was found that although some angry outbursts served no purpose, others were very helpful. One manager reported that a contractor had changed the terms and conditions on a project they were working on without getting approval first. During a meeting, the manager had an emotional outburst and let the guy know in no uncertain terms that he wasn't going to tolerate what he had done. The researchers asked if he had regretted the outburst, and the manager stated that he didn't since the issue was resolved because of it.

The study also found that the difference between the effective and regrettable acts of anger was not how angry a person got, but the context of the situation. The same manager stated that his anger caused change because people knew he meant business. He isn't the type to fly off the handle, so when he did, it signaled to them that something was seriously wrong, and it needed fixing ASAP. However, if he was the type who is always on the war path, his employees would not have taken him as seriously.

Anger also works well during negotiations and provides some leverage when people are trying to arrive at a resolution. Research has found that angry people are viewed as powerful, and they are much more likely to get what they want in comparison to the person trying to negotiate with a cheerful attitude. It is also important that your anger is genuine, or it can backfire. President Obama is probably the most laid- back president America has ever had and there is nothing intimidating about his voice. You may remember the incident in 2010 when the Gulf of Mexico got flooded with oil. In his first television appearance regarding the matter, he was his usual cool, calm and collected self. Considering the severity of the situation, the American people were not happy with his response. He later appeared on TV acting more aggressive and angry and it just didn't look right. Viewers saw straight through him and accused him of being a fake.

Anger acts as an agent of change. It was anger that transformed Martin Luther King Jr. into the most powerful civil rights leader in history. It was anger that transformed W.E.B. Dubois from a scholar to a dynamic civil rights activist. It was anger that motivated Nelson Mandela to become the first Black Prime Minister in South Africa. Altruism is born out of anger; when people get angry enough about the injustices that take place in the world, it becomes the driving force that mobilizes them to fight for change. One angry person can articulate their emotion in such a powerful way that their passion becomes infectious. It is understandable that emotions such as anger and rage have a bad reputation considering the damage they can cause when used in the wrong way. However, it is important that these emotions are evaluated in the proper context and judged accordingly.

As mentioned, most people are reactionary. When they get angry, they lash out either through their words or actions. When an angry person can feel the emotion, step back and reflect on the reasons why they are angry, it increases self-awareness. A study conducted in 1977 found that 55% of participants who had recently experienced anger felt that the emotion had a positive impact on them. One third of the respondents stated that they were able to get a better understanding of the psychological issues they were facing that triggered the emotion of anger. Making the choice to use anger in a constructive way will ultimately help you understand yourself better.

When we think of a successful relationship, the assumption is that the couple is blissfully happy, madly in love and they never have any problems. That is the media image we have been fed, but most couples will tell you that their relationship is a combination of ups and downs; and sometimes, the downs are so bad they begin to question whether their union will last. A healthy relationship is capable of navigating the murky terrain of those uncertain times because both parties know how to direct their anger in a way that will ultimately benefit the relationship instead of harm it. When a couple is experiencing underlying issues that they are not aware of, it is often expressed through anger. An emotionally aware couple will be able to step back and evaluate the real reason behind this expression. In some cases, it may be that the anger is justified, they say what they need to say, and the issue is dealt with. But in cases where an angry outburst is unjustified, it is essential that the couple spends some time investigating the root of the anger so they can resolve it.

Some experts argue that anger makes people optimistic. Looking at this statement at face value it makes no sense. Why would an angry person be optimistic? A 2003 study conducted by Lerner et al found that people who were angry about the bombing of the twin towers were more hopeful that an act of violence of that nature would not take place again in the future. Those who didn't feel angry but expressed the emotion of fear were terrified that there would be attacks again in the future. One of the main differences between fear and anger is that fear can immobilize and cause a sense of pessimism and helplessness about the future.

THE BENEFITS OF FEAR

Fear is probably one of the most destructive emotions of all. It can prevent you from achieving anything meaningful in life. Like every other emotion, you can't banish fear from your life, it will show up when it wants to. The problem with fear is that it invades places it has no right to occupy. Fear has no right to show up on your doorstep before a job interview, whispering failure into your ear. It has no right to show up when you get that idea to start your own company, and tell you there's no point in trying because you won't get past first base. Fear becomes destructive in these situations because there are no beasts trying to hunt you down and you don't need to protect yourself.

Fear doesn't understand boundaries, and when it oversteps them, you've got to put it in its place.

Here are 10 things that fear doesn't want you to know:

1. Fear is the only thing stopping you from having everything you want.
2. You are capable of doing a lot more than you think.
3. There are people who will see you as a hero or a role model once you achieve your goals.
4. Your gifts serve a purpose; the world needs them.
5. You don't need to feel bad about being happy.
6. Once you've changed your life, you will motivate others to change theirs.
7. Your age doesn't determine what you are capable of.
8. If you are determined, you can accomplish your goals.
9. You are the only person who has the right to determine whether you are qualified for the task.
10. You are your biggest critic, the negative voices in your head do not matter.

The good news is that there is a positive side to fear, and it does have its benefits when it's used in the right way. Here are some of them:

Fear creates an awareness of where you are now and where you want to be. When you refuse to allow fear to paralyze you, it will spur you into action. Fear will inspire you to become a meticulous planner; you can see the bigger picture and that's what you are afraid of. Planning gets you to look at where you are and put a strategy in place to get you where you want to go. Once the goal is broken down into smaller chunks, it becomes less threatening. Additionally, the fear of failure will encourage you to take action and ensure you are properly prepared for success in your chosen endeavor. For example, one of the most common fears is public speaking. The fear of stumbling over your words in front of a large crowd will have you practicing until you are fully confident of your abilities.

One of the acronyms for fear is 'FALSE EVIDENCE APPEARING REAL.' In other words, you have created a narrative in your head about what you are facing, and you have chosen to believe it. I like to refer to fear as anxiety's cousin because they are very similar. Going back to the public speaking example, you have no way of knowing whether you are going to trip up on your words because the event hasn't happened yet. You can't teleport yourself into the future and perform your speech. Therefore, the only evidence you have that you are going to mess up is the evidence you've created in your imagination. The problem is that you spend so much time thinking about it that you've convinced yourself it's going to happen. Hence the term 'false evidence appearing real.' Once you come to the realization that the only barrier between success and failure is the barrier you've created, you will remove it.

Some of the world's most successful companies were built on the foundation of fear. The pioneer of Apple, the late Steve Jobs, was so afraid that his company would go bankrupt he took the risk of allowing his employees to have creative control of the business. As far as he was concerned, he had nothing to lose. If there was a high likelihood the organization was going to go bankrupt, why not? Because of the risks he took during economic instability, Apple still has a competitive advantage in the technology industry today.

THE BENEFITS OF GUILT

Guilt is considered an unhealthy emotion; a socially unacceptable state of existence that should have no place in society. We guilt-trip people when we want to manipulate them to do what we want, every personal development book encourages readers to let go of the guilt, and therapists provide guilt reduction sessions. Guilt has been labeled as a negative emotion, but it has another side to it.

Andre Miller is a retired leadership consultant; he now spends his days coaching his 10-year-old son's baseball team. He speaks very passionately about an experience involving a very promising player on the team. His name was Sandeep, he was from India and came from a cricket background. But instead of using his skills on the field, Sandeep had become the team's clown and was forever messing around. Sandeep was a leader and had a profound influence on the other players, so whatever he did, they followed. It was clear that this behavior was affecting the team's performance and so Andre called a meeting with the boys. Andre didn't want to hold the meeting and was very uncomfortable with the whole scenario, which was one of the reasons why he left it for so long. He started the meeting by letting them know that he wasn't comfortable with what he was about to discuss with them.

Once he had their attention, he asked them to consider whether their behavior was beneficial or detrimental to the team. Andre gave them a minute to think about it, he then asked each team member to provide an example of how they'd helped the team that day. He then asked them to come up with an example of how they'd hurt the team previously. After they had all spoken, Andre explained to the boys that one person's bad behavior had a negative effect on everyone, but instead of feeling bad about it, now was the time to do something about it.

Afterwards, Andre had a conversation with Sandeep and explained that he would no longer be the star player, and that he would have to sit on the bench for a couple of games. Sandeep understood and accepted the punishment, but when he was put back in position, he played like he had never played before, and the team won their first game of the season. Sandeep got more respect from his teammates for getting a win than he did for his silly antics. When he realized this, his attitude completely changed. Andre wasn't just a coach, he was helping these young boys transition into responsible teenagers, and by opening up about his own discomfort, and making them feel slightly guilty, he had succeeded in getting them on the right track. The question "Is what you are doing helping or hurting..." is a powerful one; it forces you to evaluate your behavior in the right context. If it's helping, continue; if it's hurting, stop.

World renowned clinical psychologist June Tangney has been studying guilt in criminals for decades. She found that the criminals who felt guilty about the crimes they had committed were more likely to apologize, confess or try and fix the wrongs they had committed. Additionally, the criminals who had been sentenced to prison were less likely to commit another crime when they were released, and therefore, less likely to return to prison.

Feeling guilty appears to add to our moral fiber and motivates us to be more considerate and socially sensitive citizens. For example, research has discovered that people who feel guilty are less likely to assault someone, use illegal drugs, steal or drive under the influence. If our true character is only determined by the things we do when we are alone and no one is looking, you can argue that the moral emotion of guilt is a beneficial one.

THE BENEFITS OF SADNESS

If you had the choice, you would choose happiness over sadness, right? I don't blame you, I would too and I think the majority of the world would also. The word 'happiness' is tossed around like confetti; everywhere you turn someone is trying to sell you a book or a course on how to find true and lasting happiness, which is great, but the reality is that it doesn't exist. Not to sound pessimistic but life simply won't allow it because stuff happens, and there are a lot of things in life that can make you feel sad. The good news is that even though sadness doesn't feel good, it does have its benefits.

I felt sad a couple of days ago when my best friend told me she was moving to another state to pursue her dreams. I told her I was happy for her, and we had an exciting conversation about the move. But as soon as I got off the phone, I started feeling sad; I mean, she's my best friend, we've spent the best part of ten years in each other's pockets, and now she's going away! I had every reason to be sad, but my immediate reaction was to try and alleviate the feeling and return to a happy state, and that isn't how you reap the benefits of sadness.

A study published by the British Psychological Society reported the cultural differences in the attitudes about sadness between Germans and Americans. When analyzing sympathy cards, it was found that Americans write positive messages that encourage people not to focus on their grief such as, *"There is light at the end of the tunnel,"* whereas Germans wrote messages such as, *"You have experienced a great loss, take as much time as you need to heal."* The study highlighted the fact that American culture would rather avoid than embrace sadness. In contrast, the German culture embraces sadness and doesn't focus on the light at the end of the tunnel; instead, they prefer to sit and look at the dark walls until they are ready to move forward. According to clinical psychologist Dr. Noam Shpancer, avoiding negative emotions only provides short-term relief. Eventually, the sadness you were trying to avoid will resurface.

The *Journal of Experimental Social Psychology* published a study about persuasion and sadness. The study involved participants watching a happy or sad movie. After watching the movie, they were given the task of writing a persuasive essay about a controversial topic. The researchers discovered that participants who watched the sad movie wrote the most persuasive essays. One of the main reasons for this is that negative emotions encourage critical thinking and improve focus.

THE BENEFITS OF ANXIETY

Anxiety is a common emotion, and a lot has been written about it. When people are too anxious, it's overwhelming; but a little bit of anxiety can be helpful. For example, it helps drive success in areas of career, family and romance. Additionally, there are some situations in which anxiety is necessary because it works as a human alarm system and alerts us to problems. Here are some of the things that anxious people do best:

- They don't like feeling anxious; therefore, they will work on a problem until it's resolved. Even if it means losing sleep or going without food; their number one priority is fixing the issue.
- They are investigators, so when they feel that something isn't right, they will devote all their time and energy into proving that their 'off' feeling was valid.
- They sense danger very quickly, so being with them guarantees your safety.
- They pay attention to their surroundings; they are always on high alert, so changes in things like smell and sound are picked up quickly.

You absolutely do not want to suffer from chronic anxiety, and nor do you want a workforce or a household of people who are always anxious. But having no anxiety whatsoever can also be detrimental. One study involved a group of participants being led to believe that they had triggered a virus that destroyed important computer files. They had to find the owner of the computer and explain to them what happened. On their way, there were several obstacles designed to prevent them from reaching the owner of the computer. To overcome these obstacles, they had to be assertive and abrupt. The most anxious people became extremely focused, made their way through the obstacles and completed the task.

In conclusion, many of us thought they were superheroes with a superpower when we were children. You might have thought you could fly, had superhuman strength or maybe you had laser vision. You can also view your emotions as a superpower. When you take into consideration all the positive and negative benefits your emotions bring, you don't just have one superpower, you have several. Anger can give you courage, guilt makes you think twice about unethical behavior and anxiety keeps you safe. The bottom line is that people are prejudiced against negative emotional experiences because of the labels that society has attached to them, and because people often view them through the lens of the more extreme form of the emotion. Anxiety is misrepresented as a panic attack, anger is confused with rage, and guilt is viewed through the lens of shame. In other words, some emotions are only viewed through the lens of negativity.

If you want to reap the benefits of negative emotions, it's important that you know how to manage them. In the next chapter, you will learn exactly how to do this.

CHAPTER 7

HOW TO MANAGE NEGATIVE EMOTIONS

Managing negative emotions is a common problem for many people. Have you ever noticed that when someone starts crying in front of you, the first thing they do is put their head down and apologize? As mentioned several times throughout this book, one of the main reasons for this cover-up and shame is that society hasn't learned to embrace the full spectrum of emotions. But if you are going to live a fulfilling life, it is essential that you learn to manage negative emotions. Due to space constraints, it is impossible to cover all negative emotions in this chapter, and so I have focused on the most common ones: anger, fear, anxiety, stress and sadness.

HOW TO MANAGE ANGER

Anger management is crucial to your emotional wellbeing. You read in Chapter 6 how anger is beneficial, but only if it's channeled in the right way. Additionally, there are different types or levels of anger. For example, it is highly unlikely that getting angry with your boyfriend for forgetting to take the trash out is going to drive you to become the next Nelson Mandela. But the anger from being falsely accused of a crime and sentenced to prison might. Your anger might involve getting frustrated while sitting in traffic, or lashing out at someone because they stole your parking spot, or getting into arguments with your colleagues at work. When left to fester, angry feelings can lead to aggressive behavior such as having a screaming match, fighting or damaging property. Some people don't express their anger outwardly, but instead they internalize it, and as you have read, this can have a negative effect on your health. Anger management is about learning how to recognize, express and cope with your anger in a productive and healthy way. Here are some strategies to effectively manage your anger:

Identify Triggers: If you are known for your anger, you likely have a habit of losing your temper. If you have a bad temper, there are things that will trigger it such as excessive tiredness, sarcastic comments, traffic jams and long queues. Recognizing your triggers is not about blaming people or making excuses for your behavior, it's about recognizing the things that set you off so you can work around them. There are some triggers you can't avoid such as heavy traffic after work, but anger management strategies will give you the tools you need to prepare yourself before entering into a situation that will prevent you from getting angry.

Analyze Your Anger: Before you express your anger, calm yourself down and ask yourself whether your anger is constructive or deconstructive. For example, are you angry because your friend took too long to go to the store? Or are you angry because your friend's rights have been violated and you want to make things right? In both instances your anger could be an indication that you need to make a change. For example, getting angry because your friend took too long to go to the store may be a sign that there are underlying issues in your relationship, and you need to have a conversation with your friend about it. And if your friend's rights have been violated, maybe you need to work with them to ensure that something is done to rectify the situation. In these scenarios, your anger is a friend because it has given you a warning that something isn't right. However, if your anger is damaging your relationships and causing you distress, then your anger is your enemy. Signs that anger is your enemy include regretting what you have said or done after the fact and feeling as if you have no control. In this situation, you will need to employ one or more of the anger management strategies mentioned in this section.

Pay Attention to Warning Signs: People who find it difficult to control their temper often describe their anger as 'coming out of nowhere.' One minute they are fine, the next they are having an outburst. But if you stop and pay attention for a second, you will find that there are warning signs alerting you to the fact that you are about to get angry. Have you ever driven into a dead end and then when you turned around and went back the way you came, realized that there was a big warning sign letting you know you were about to drive into a dead end? It's not that the sign wasn't there, you just missed it because you were preoccupied with something else. Anger warning signs work in the same way. You become so preoccupied with the situation that has made you angry, that you react without thinking about it. As mentioned at the beginning of this section, anger management isn't about not getting angry, it's about managing the anger when it arises, so it's important that you are cognizant of the fact that your efforts are not about *not* getting angry. I stress this because people tend to feel guilty about getting angry, but don't focus on that, focus on managing the anger.

One of the most common warning signs for anger is a physical change in the body. People in abusive relationships often state that they know when to make a run for it because they will notice the physical changes in their partner. Their face may get red, they start sweating, they start clenching their fists or their breathing intensifies. You may react differently; for example, you might experience cognitive changes such as seeing red or having racing thoughts. Nevertheless, whatever your physical reactions, pay attention to them because they are like an alarm bell and provide you with the opportunity to take the action required to prevent you from doing or saying something you will regret later.

Remove Yourself from the Situation: Trying to prove a point only serves to fuel your anger. If you are having a discussion with someone that starts getting heated because you are in disagreement, step back. There is no point in enforcing your opinions on people because if they don't agree, they don't agree. I am not suggesting that you refrain from getting your point across all the time. But only do so when you and the person you are communicating with are in a healthy emotional state. You will know whether this is the case because you are both willing to listen to each other's opinions, you are not having a shouting match, and you might even feel like you are learning something new. On the other hand, whether you are in a meeting at work, or having a discussion with your partner, when things start getting heated, excuse yourself and take a walk. If you always get into arguments with your partner, talk to them about this. Let your significant other know that you are working on your anger management and when temperatures start rising, you will need to go for a walk, and you will return to finish the conversation when you've calmed down. In this way, you are letting them know that you are not walking away from coming to a resolution, but that you need space to clear your mind. Additionally, you can set a time to continue the conversation with your partner, friend or work colleague so that you all have peace that the issue is not going to be left unresolved.

Talk to Someone: If you have a friend or a relative who is easy to talk to, get on the phone and speak to them when you feel anger rising. People like this typically have a high level of emotional intelligence, they are able to see things from your point of view, but at the same time get you to look at your situation from a different perspective. Empathetic people have a calming effect on you because they will allow you to express your feelings without saying things that are going to offend you or fuel your anger. Additionally, it's important to understand that you are not to use friends or family members as sounding boards. Speaking to someone is not about venting by screaming at them so that you don't scream at the person you are angry with. It's about expressing yourself in healthy way with the aim of finding a solution to your problem.

Research suggests that venting by yelling or smashing things can actually make you angrier because you are focusing too much on the situation that has made you angry instead of looking for a solution.

Physical Activity: One of the hormones that surge through the body when you get angry is adrenaline. One of the most effective ways to use that energy is to engage in physical activity.

When that feeling arises, go for a run, a brisk walk or go to the gym. This will help burn off the tension. Additionally, regular exercise is a good way to decompress and reduce stress. It can also help you build up your tolerance for frustration. You will also find that exercise is a great way to clear your mind, and after a good workout, you are able to come up with a viable solution to your problem.

Manage Your Thinking: Thought control is very difficult to achieve, but it's possible. One of ways anger manifests is through negative thinking. You may find yourself in a situation and instead of thinking about it rationally, you automatically think the worst. For example, you walk in on your partner having a conversation with her friend. She is discussing what a friend might wear to attract the attention of the guy she is dating. When you walk into the room, all you hear is, *"I think wearing figure-hugging clothes that are not too revealing is a great way to attract his attention."* You immediately feel uncomfortable and assume that she is talking about what she can wear to attract the attention of someone other than her boyfriend, and that's the only direction your thoughts are taking. You keep turning this idea over and over in your head and so by the time she gets off the phone, you've reached boiling point and you are ready to go to war. When you think about it, you've basically made yourself angry by drawing your own conclusions about what you've heard.

Thinking about this situation in a rational manner would involve you reminding yourself that you know what you've just heard, but you trust your girlfriend and she's not the type to cheat. Therefore, there is no point in thinking anything negative; instead, think about all the good times you have had in your relationship. When she gets off the phone, have a casual conversation about what she was talking about with her friend so that she doesn't get defensive and feel like you are accusing her of being unfaithful. Additionally, you can develop a mantra such as, *"I am calm and peaceful right now,"* repeating this continuously until you feel the anger subsiding.

Focus on Something Else: Focusing on something else is similar to changing the way you think. When something bad happens, we have a tendency to replay the incident over and over again in our minds. For example, if you went to the store, and the assistant spoke to you in a way you didn't like, you will spend the trip home going over aspects of her behavior. From the way she rolled her eyes, to the tone of her voice and everything in between. Instead of focusing on the injustice you think you've experienced, focus on something else. The easiest way to shift gears is to do something challenging. If you are at home, you might get a jigsaw puzzle out, play with the kids or pay some bills. When you find something to do that will keep your mind occupied, you will notice that your mind and body will calm down.

Don't Make Assumptions: In the book 7 *Habits of Highly Effective People* by Stephen Covey, he discusses an incident that took place on a train. He was on his way somewhere, the train was quiet but quite packed, everyone seemed to be in their own world either reading, listening to music, or just sitting. At one stop, a man got on with his three children. The man sat next to Covey and the three children went off doing their own thing. The children were extremely loud, yelling, running up and down and bumping into people. You could see that passengers were getting visibly annoyed, huffing, puffing and tutting in hope that the man would take control of his children, but he just sat there completely oblivious to what was going on. After a while, Covey politely turned to the man and asked if he would mind keeping his children under control. The man looked into the distance and apologized, and then went onto say, "Perhaps I should, but we have just come back from the hospital to be told that their mother has just died, and I don't think they really know what to do." Covey's entire attitude towards the man changed immediately.

The moral of the story here is that you never know what burdens people are carrying. The cashier who gave you attitude may suffer from depression, the person who cut you off might be driving their sick mother to the hospital. The person who mindlessly bumped into you in the street could have just been diagnosed with cancer. So before you get angry with someone, remind yourself that you have no idea whether the weight of the burden they are carrying has driven them to act in a way that has offended you.

Explore Your Feelings: As mentioned earlier, anger can either be your friend or your enemy because it's either helping you or harming you. I want you to go back to that with this strategy and think about what else your anger is trying to tell you. Sometimes anger acts as a protective mask that you use to avoid other emotions such as disappointment, sadness and embarrassment. For example, a friend or a work colleague might give you feedback that you find difficult to hear. The feeling of embarrassment might make you lash out in anger because you have convinced yourself that the person giving the feedback has a vendetta against you when the reality is that they are trying to help you. Creating the narrative that the person is unfairly criticizing you will make you feel better temporarily because you are not focused on the embarrassment. However, dealing with underlying emotions will help you get to the root of the problem.

For example, let's say you've invited your sister to your graduation ceremony and she cancels on you at the last minute. The underlying emotion is probably disappointment, but to hide this, you express anger. You can deal with the underlying emotion of disappointment by having an honest discussion with her about it. In this way, your sister gets a better understanding about how you feel, and you haven't damaged the relationship with an angry outburst.

Make a 'Calm Down' Box: Maybe you come home from work frustrated and irritated and take it out on out on your family members. Or you know that certain work meetings can aggravate you. Instead of succumbing to the anger, create a calm down box that will help you relax. Things that engage your senses can create a calming effect on the mind. So your calm down box might include a spiritual message, a picture of the sun setting on the beach, your favorite candy, a motivational speech to listen to or scented hand lotion. Whatever makes you feel calm, include those things in your box and take it everywhere you go. You can also store instructions for breathing exercises or guided mediations in a folder on your phone.

Get Professional Help: If after some time, you find that these strategies are not working for you, get some professional help. You may have a deeper issue that you are unaware of. There are several mental health issues that are linked to aggressive outbursts such as depression and post-traumatic stress disorder. Start by talking to your healthcare practitioner about your behavior and moods. They will make sure you don't have a physical condition that is contributing to the problem. Your doctor can also refer you to a mental health professional for a thorough examination. Depending on your needs and goals, the treatment might include anger management classes as well as individual sessions.

HOW TO MANAGE STRESS

Stress is a normal part of life; taking care of children, working on relationships, and studying for exams are all things that can cause stress in your life and sometimes they can become too difficult to manage. Since you can't run away from these responsibilities, the assumption is that there is nothing you can do about it, but there is plenty you can do to regain control over your life and relieve the pressure associated with stressful circumstances. Stress management is important because, like all other negative emotions, stress can have a detrimental effect on your emotional and physical wellbeing if it's not managed effectively. Stress stifles your ability to function effectively, think clearly, and enjoy life the way you want to. When it comes to stress, it's important to understand that there are always going to be 24 hours in a day; no matter how much you want to extend time, that is one thing you will never be able to do. The bills are going to keep coming, you are always going to have family and work-related responsibilities – none of this will stop. The only thing you can change is how you manage the stress in your life.

The aim of stress management is to break the hold that it has over your life so you can be more productive, healthier and happier. The ultimate goal is to achieve and maintain a balance which allows you time for work, family, friends, leisure and relaxation. Balance will give you the resilience you need to keep going when it feels as if life is spinning out of control. However, it's important to understand that there is no "one size fits all" when it comes to stress management. What works for you might not work for others; therefore, it's important to find the most effective strategies and stick to them.

Where is the Stress Coming From? Identifying the source of your stress is not always easy to determine because there are several factors that contribute to chronic stress. You won't have a problem identifying major stressors such as a negative health diagnosis, separating from your spouse, moving to a new house or apartment or changing jobs. The difficulty is in evaluating how your own behaviors, thoughts and feelings are contributing to your stress levels. For example, you might find that you are always stressed about meeting work deadlines, but the real problem isn't the deadlines, it's the fact that you spend too much time procrastinating. To identify the root cause of your stress, analyze your attitude, habits and excuses:

- Do you make justifications for your stress, such as, *"I've got a million things to do at the moment"* while ignoring the fact that you never take a break?
- Do you accept extreme stress as normal? You might attribute it to your personality and make statements such as, *"I've just got a lot of nervous energy at the moment,"* or *"This house is always crazy"*?
- Do you blame stress on outside events or other people?

When it comes to stress management, the first step is to take responsibility for playing an active role in maintaining or creating the stress in your life. Once you accept that your stress levels are not outside your control, you will find it easier to manage them.

Stress Management and the 4 As: Your nervous system is responsible for your automatic response to stress. However, in some instances, you know when stress is going to become a problem, for example, at family gatherings, a meeting with your manager, or your commute to work. When dealing with stressors you can predict, you can either change your response, or change the situation; this is where the four As of *avoid, alter, adapt* and *accept* come in handy.

Avoid Stressful Situations: When a stressful situation needs to be addressed, don't avoid it, but eliminate other stressors in your life by doing the following:

- *Task Elimination:* Evaluate your schedule, tasks, and daily responsibilities. If you've got too much to manage, either put some of your least important tasks at the bottom of the list or remove them.
- *Change Your Environment:* Is your work area so untidy that you find it difficult to focus? Clean it. Does going to the grocery store frustrate you? Shop online. Does traffic make you angry? Take a route where there's less traffic, even if it takes longer. Does the TV news make you anxious? Stop watching it.
- *Avoid Negative People:* Is there someone in your life who causes you constant stress? If you can end the relationship, do so. If not, keep them at arm's length.
- *Say No:* Saying no will alleviate a lot of pressure and free up some of your time. There is no need to agree to attend every social event or say yes to every extra project your manager asks you to take on. If you can't do it, just say no.

Alter the Situation: You can change the situation if you can't avoid it; this will involve changing the way you operate and communicate in your daily life.

- *Balance Your Schedule:* Balance out your schedule and stick to it. Block out time for family, friends and leisure and refuse to compromise.
- *Be Open to Change:* If you are dealing with another person and the only way to come to an amicable solution is to make some behavioral changes, then that is what you are going to need to do.
- *Express Your Feelings:* Internalizing your feelings is a recipe for disaster. Assertiveness is required if you are going to eliminate unnecessary stress from your life. If you find someone annoying, let them know without being disrespectful. If you need to study for an exam and your roommate is a bit on the noisy side, ask them to keep it down. If you don't speak up, you will build up resentment and this increases stress in your life.

Adapt to the Situation: There are some stressors that you can't change, so in such instances, focus on changing yourself and not the stressor.

- *Eliminate Perfection:* There is no such thing as perfection, it doesn't exist. Demanding perfection sets you up for failure; this is especially true when it comes to other people. Excellence is a powerful trait, but there are times when 'good enough' will have to do.
- *Evaluate the Bigger Picture:* A lot of things we get stressed out about are temporary. In a month's time, they will no

longer matter; evaluate the situation from a long-term perspective before you form a judgment.

- *Reframe the Problem:* Instead of getting stressed out about a situation, find something positive about it. For example, if you are frustrated because you are stuck in a traffic jam, see it as an opportunity to listen to your latest audio book, or to catch up with an old friend.

- *Practice Gratitude:* When stress starts taking over, take a moment to step back and think about all the things in your life you've got to be grateful for.

Accept the Things You Can't Control: There are some stressful situations that you have no control over. A national recession, the death of a loved one, or the diagnosis of a terminal illness are a few of the many life problems that you are powerless to control. Such situations are never easy to deal with, but ultimately, it's better than battling with a situation you can't change.

- *Look for the Benefits:* Negative situations can be about personal growth if you want them to be. Sometimes, your own poor decisions can cause stressful situations. If this is the case, learn from the mistake, move on and don't repeat it.

- *Relinquish Control:* When you know there is nothing you can do to control a situation, let it go. This is especially true when it comes to the behavior of others. You can't control how someone chooses to behave, but you can control how you respond to their behavior.

- *Speak to Someone:* Talking about how you feel is very cathartic. When you know you can't control the situation, it's not about speaking to someone to find a solution, it's about releasing your negative emotions. Just make sure you are speaking to the right person such as a trusted family member, friend or therapist.

- *Forgiveness:* If someone has caused you painful offense, let it go. Forgive the person and get on with your life. Unforgiveness is a dangerous emotion because the only person it destroys is you.

Physical Activity: As you've read, physical activity is good for all negative emotions because of the feel- good hormones it releases into the body. Additionally, it can serve as an important distraction from many of the stressful situations you go through in life. The long-term benefits come from a consistent daily exercise routine. However, it's all about getting started. Here are several ways you can get moving without doing a full workout:

- Park your car a few streets away from your location and walk
- Use the stairs instead of the elevator
- Play an activity-based video game
- Cycle or walk to the grocery store
- Start taking your dog for walks
- Put some music on and dance around the house

Connect with People: There is nothing more refreshing than spending quality time with the people you love and care about. Positive people who uplift your spirits and remind you that there is more to your life than the stress you are currently facing. Face-to-face interaction is always better than over the phone or through a Zoom or Skype call. Building and maintaining a network of close friends is essential for stress management. Here are a few tips on how to do this:

- Join a club or take a class to meet new people
- Schedule dinner dates with a friend once a week/month
- Take a walk with your workout partner
- Email or call an old friend
- Make a movie or concert date with a friend
- Schedule a coffee or lunch date with a work colleague every week/month
- Become a volunteer

Make Time for Relaxation and Fun: Outside of a positive attitude and a take-charge approach, a powerful stress reduction strategy is to make time for yourself. Forget friends and family for a moment, it's all about you! It's easy to get so caught up with the hustle and bustle of life that you forget about nurturing yourself and taking care of your own needs. If you are a parent or a single mother, don't feel guilty about doing this, because when you're not okay, it becomes even more difficult to take care of others. Additionally, when you make time to have fun and relax, you will find it easier to handle the stress that life throws at you.

Take a Break: You can decide when you are going to do this, but every day, set aside time to relax. I don't mean lunch or dinner time; just take a break from everything for an hour and do nothing!

Maintain a Sense of Humor: Laughter is like medicine to the soul. Find something to laugh about daily. You can do this by watching your favorite comedian or reading some jokes from a joke book. Regardless of how you choose to do it, make sure you have one big belly laugh a day.

Practice Relaxation: Activities such as meditation, yoga and breathing exercises are effective relaxation techniques. Make a habit of practicing one of them every day.

Do Something You Enjoy: Whether it's reading, star gazing, or playing the piano, make the time to do something you enjoy every day.

Improve Your Time Management: Waking up late, spending two hours straightening your hair or just procrastinating in general will increase your stress levels. It's difficult to stay focused and calm when you are always in a rush. Additionally, when you are pushed for time, you tend to cut back on the things that are good for you such as exercising, healthy eating and getting enough sleep. Here are a few tips on how to manage your time effectively:

- *Delegate:* Are there things you can give to your partner, children or employees to do? When you feel overwhelmed, start handing out projects.
- *Prioritize:* Because the brain likes being comfortable, we often put off the most difficult tasks until the end. This is not a good idea, and it is one of the reasons why a lot of your tasks on your to-do list don't get done. Get the most difficult things out of the way *first* because that is when you have the most energy. You will feel less stressed knowing that you have completed the most burdensome projects.

- *Break it Down:* When you've got a large project to complete, break it down into small manageable chunks so you won't feel so overwhelmed and keep putting it off.

Quick Stress Relief: The above strategies are a great way to manage stress over the long term, but stress relief in the moment is equally as important. You might feel exhausted from your 2-hour morning commute, being stuck in a high-tension work meeting, or frustrated because of an argument with your partner. During times like this, you need quick stress relief so that it doesn't interfere with the rest of your day. Here are some tips to eliminate stress immediately:

- *Chew Gum:* Sounds strange but according to research, it works. Apparently, vigorous chewing will help you release pent-up frustration.
- *Have a Cup of Tea:* If you are in a place where you can make a cup of tea, do so because it will help calm you down. The act of drinking tea is also helpful because it's warm and comforting.
- *Inhale Essential Oils:* Inhaling essential oils is known as aromatherapy and it helps reduce anxiety and calm the mind. You can place a few droplets of an essential oil on a rag and carry it around. When you feel stressed, take it out and inhale deeply for 10 minutes. Popular oils for relieving stress include orange blossom, ylang ylang, sandalwood, frankincense, Roman chamomile, bergamot, vetiver, rose and lavender.
- *Stretching:* Stretching is a simple way to relieve the body of tension. Whether you are sitting at your desk or stuck in traffic, when you start feeling stressed, give your body a stretch and you will feel a lot better.

- *4-7-8 Breathing Method:* This powerful breathing exercise gives your body an additional shot of oxygen. Deep breathing works well to reduce anxiety, depression and stress.
    - Position the tip of your tongue on the roof of your mouth and leave it there throughout the exercise.
    - Slightly part your lips and exhale through your mouth at the same time as making a whooshing sound.
    - Close your lips and quietly breathe in through your nose while counting to 4.
    - Hold your breath for a count of 7.
    - Breathe out for 8 seconds and make a swooshing sound.
    - Complete the cycle 4 times.

- **Emotional Freedom Technique (EFT):** This is also known as psychological acupressure or tapping. EFT originates from traditional Chinese medicine and it involves tapping certain energy centers of the body while repeating mantras that will help you acknowledge the problems you are having at the same time as learning to accept yourself.
    - Identify where the stress is coming from.
    - On a scale of 1-10, describe the level of stress you feel.
    - Make up a mantra that addresses the problem. For example, *"Even though figuring out how I'm going to pay this bill is stressing me out, I choose to completely and deeply love and accept myself."*
    - There are nine energy centers (also known as meridian points): under the arm, at the top of the

collarbone, the chin, under the nose, under the eyes, the side of the eyes, and eyebrow. Tap on these areas seven times each and repeat the phrase each time you tap on a point.

— Once you have finished, rate your stress level, and if it's gone down, you're fine; if not, do it again.

• **Third Person Conversation:** Having a conversation with a friend about a stressful situation is therapeutic. However, there are times when no one is around and the only person you can speak to is yourself. In such instances, the best way to address the conversation is to speak in third person. Having a third person conversation helps you control negative emotions. Experts claim that speaking to yourself in the third person helps people think about themselves in the same way they think about others. Additionally, it helps distance yourself from the situation.

HOW TO MANAGE FEAR AND ANXIETY

Anxiety is a form of fear, and the strategies to overcome fear and anxiety are very similar which is why I've put them together. When we experience fear and anxiety often, they will stifle us and prevent us from living a fulfilling life which is why you should take authority over them now. Here are some strategies to help you overcome fear and anxiety:

Awareness of Your Fear: This is going to be extremely difficult to establish because you've probably spent the majority of your life avoiding it. However, if you want to overcome it, you've got to confront it. Fear is often rooted in the unknown; we are afraid of what we think it can do, and not of what we know it can do. Facing your fear means gaining awareness of it. So now it's onto your research phase; get Googling and reading, find out as much as you can about your fear.

Positive Imagination: When you are afraid of something, you think the worst. You spend your time imagining all the terrible things that might happen if you were to get into the situation. The operative word here is 'might.' There is no guarantee that this fear is going to manifest because you've just imagined it will and those thoughts have put you in a state of fear. You can reverse this by thinking about a positive outcome. Let's say you're afraid of public speaking. The company you work for always asks you to speak, but you keep getting out of it by claiming you are ill a couple of days before the event. The main reason you're so afraid of speaking in front of an audience is that you imagine yourself making a complete fool of yourself. Instead, imagine yourself doing a fantastic job and getting a standing ovation.

Practice: Fear and anxiety are both rooted in a fear of failure, and you are afraid you are going to fail because you don't feel confident about it. Let's use the public speaking example again. You can build your confidence in public speaking by practicing. You can take a course, speak in front of the mirror or record yourself speaking. Once you gain more confidence, the fear and anxiety will decrease.

Focus on Your Breathing: Breathing is very important and experts state that anxious and fearful people are shallow breathers. They take short, shallow breaths which causes the body to react in a negative way. If you've ever had a panic attack, you will know that one of the symptoms is your inability to breathe. One way to control your anxiety is by taking control of your breathing. Box breathing is one of the most effective breathing techniques to overcome anxiety, so it is used by Navy Seals when entering into a stressful situation.

- Inhale deeply from the stomach all the way to the chest and count to 4.
- Hold your breath for 4 seconds.
- Breathe into your stomach and count to 4.
- Hold your breath for 4 seconds and repeat.

Repeat the exercise until the anxiety disappears. You can perform this breathing exercise any time you feel anxious, no matter where you are.

Practice Mindfulness: When you recognize the symptoms of anxiety, take a step back and evaluate why you are feeling this way. Focus on the symptoms as they arise and don't try and control them, just monitor yourself as they happen. This process raises your self-awareness and prevents you from doing what you would normally do when you get into a fearful state.

Observe Nature: Going for a walk and paying attention to nature helps reduce feelings of anxiety. Look up at the sky, down at the grass, or smell a flower. Nature has a calming effect and will help reduce anxiety-related symptoms.

How to Manage Sadness

Sadness is a powerful emotion, it should be felt, embraced, and managed in the right way to prevent people from getting stuck in a permanent state of sadness.

Give Yourself Permission to Feel Sad: Giving yourself permission to feel sad is not the same as giving in to the sadness and allowing it to drag you into depression. As mentioned earlier, people often apologize when they start crying in front of someone. If something has upset you, you have the right to feel your pain. Acknowledge how you feel, don't put on a fake smile to appease people, don't deny yourself the opportunity to heal by suppressing your sadness.

Cry: Research suggests that emotional tears have several health benefits. To begin with, tears contain high levels of the stress hormone cortisol, and they also contain high levels of the mood-regulating hormone manganese. Additionally, crying tightens the muscles, and this helps to release some of the tension you are feeling. Studies have also found that crying triggers the parasympathetic nervous system which helps the body become balanced again. Crying is so beneficial that some places in Japan have built crying clubs called 'rui-katsu', which means 'tear-seeking.' People gather there for one reason and one reason only, and that is to cry. Here are some of the health benefits associated with crying:

- *Dulls Pain:* Long crying spells release the feel-good hormones endorphins and oxytocin; they can help ease both emotional and physical pain. When the endorphins are released, the body goes into a state of numbness, and the oxytocin has a calming effect.
- *Recovery from Grief:* Grief happens in various stages, and crying is one of them. Crying is a very important stage in the grieving process because it helps you process and accept loss.

- *Improves Sleep:* A 2015 study discovered that crying helps babies sleep better. As mentioned, emotional tears contain high levels of the stress hormone cortisol. Therefore, when the babies in the research group were left to cry at night, they released more of the stress hormone and this put them in a relaxed state, enabling them to sleep better.

Talk About it: In psychology, discussing your problems is referred to as talking therapy. During one-on-one sessions with a counselor, the patient talks about their problems while the counselor listens. Whether a solution is found depends on the individual circumstances but the aim is to releases the emotion. You don't need to see a therapist to talk to someone about what you are going through. A trusted friend or family member who is willing to listen without casting judgment can be equally as helpful.

Creative Expression: Are you a dancer, poet or musician? Sadness is a powerful motivator for creativity. Some of the world's best works were developed during times of great sadness. The Sistine Chapel by Michelangelo was a monumental achievement, but in his letters, he indicates that he painted the work in a state of exhaustion and depression. The song 'Now I'm In It' by Haim was written by the lead singer Danielle Haim. She states that the song was her opening up about her battle with depression. 'Help' by the Beatles was also about depression, as John Lennon stated that he was bitterly depressed during that time and the song was literally his cry for help.

Now that you know how to manage your negative emotions, the final stage is to maintain good emotional health.

CHAPTER 8

HOW TO MAINTAIN GOOD EMOTIONAL HEALTH

Good emotional health is just as important as good physical health. As you have read, they are connected, and when one is in bad condition, so is the other. Improving your emotional health isn't going to happen overnight, so if you suffer from trapped emotions, emotional numbness or other types of emotional trauma, you will need to spend time working through those issues. But you can still work on maintaining good emotional health at the same time. The following strategies will get you started:

LEARN TO GUIDE YOUR EMOTIONS

I don't know about you, but I enjoy being comfortable. I like the comfort of my bed, of certain clothes. I take comfort in being around predictable people, whether it's family, friends or co-workers. I struggle when it comes to doing things that take me out of my comfort zone and that includes my emotions. But as I've traveled on this journey of self-discovery, I've learned that growth requires stepping out of your comfort zone, and that includes your emotions.

You can induce your emotions if you so desire, but not on an extreme level. For example, if I feel sad, I can think about something funny and laugh, but it's not going to remove the sadness; it will return after I've laughed. We are often given this advice by well-meaning friends when we are going through feelings of depression, anxiety or hopelessness... *"Just think positive and things will work out in the end."* It's all well and good to 'think positive,' but that's not enough. However, you can make a gradual transition from one emotion to the other. The Emotional Guidance Scale is a concept pioneered by Ether and Jerry Hicks, and it describes how our emotions shift from one vibration to the next. The scale is divided into the most common emotions with joy having the highest vibration, and powerlessness the lowest. In between there are emotions such as passion, enthusiasm, boredom and doubt.

You can compare the emotional guidance scale to climbing a ladder. Unless you are Superman, if you are at the bottom of the ladder, you can't just catapult yourself to the top. You've got to climb up it one rung at a time. Likewise, when you are not in the best of moods, you can slowly climb up the emotional scale until you get to the top. The key is to wait until you feel stable in one emotion before moving to the next. Here are the steps you will need to take:

STEP 1: WHAT EMOTION ARE YOU FEELING?

Take a look at the emotional guidance scale and decide which emotion you can identify with the most.

STEP 2: BE KIND TO YOURSELF

As mentioned, we live in a world where negative emotions are not celebrated. In general, we have been conditioned to hate dealing with them, even in other people. When you call a friend to talk about your problems and they give you advice such as, "You need to be a bit more positive, babe," what they are really trying to say is, "Shut the hell up, I don't want to hear about your problems, I've got my own junk to deal with." The way the world views negative emotions is the reason why you beat yourself up when you aren't feeling upbeat and energetic. As you read in Chapter 6, negative emotions serve a purpose when they are channeled in the right direction. There is nothing wrong with feeling depressed, scared, anxious or angry; the emotion isn't the problem, your reaction is.

Once you've acknowledged the emotion you are feeling, don't guilt yourself for feeling that way, you are more than entitled to feel how you feel. Be thankful that you've got the capacity to experience emotions and that you can recognize what they are when they surface. At this point you can say an affirmation. To prepare yourself for the emotional shift, say something like: *"Thank you for allowing me to feel and experience these feelings. I am grateful that I have the ability to acknowledge that I am not in alignment with my power, but I now choose to leave this frequency and increase my vibration."*

Step 3: Choose another emotion

If you are feeling anger, the next emotion on the emotional scale is discouragement. How do you shift from anger to discouragement? You remember what made you angry. For example, say your partner made you angry because they were late to your work gathering. The problem isn't that they were late, but that they are late for everything and he/she promised you that they would make more of an effort, but they failed. You can induce feelings of discouragement by thinking about how badly you've been disappointed, and you can't see them ever changing. Get comfortable in the emotion of discouragement and then move on to the next.

STEP 4: KEEP GOING

It might take a couple of days, months or years to reach the feeling of joy. But the aim is to keep inducing your emotions until you get there. Every time you move up the scale, reward yourself. The higher you climb, the easier it will become. It's easy to get stuck in one emotion and remain there, but it's difficult to make the conscious decision to move up the scale until you experience joy. As with all things that are beneficial for you, they take time to master, so keep practicing.

EMOTIONAL MUSCLE MEMORY

When you are learning to ride a bike for the first time, you are very aware of your actions because you've got to concentrate. You are in a state of hypervigilance because you know you don't have full control over what you are doing. You are trying to think about everything at once: the speed you are going, the road you are on, how to hold the handlebars and everything else that goes into riding a bike. The more you practice, the better you become at it because the process is being stored in your muscle memory. While you are sleeping, your brain rehearses what you've learned and you will notice that you keep getting better. Soon, you start riding the bike without thinking about it because the technique has been perfectly stored in your muscle memory.

The same is true with any physical skill. People learning to play a musical instrument, learning to dance or swim practice the same moves over and over again until they have been stored so deeply in the muscle memory that it becomes a part of them. People like Tiger Woods, Michael Jordan and the Williams sisters are known as experts because they've spent so many years practicing that they have mastered their craft. Do you know anyone who is angry, frustrated and stressed out all the time? That's because there is also such thing as emotional memory, and these people have become experts at expressing negative emotions because they've practiced it so much it has been stored in their muscle memory. These negative emotions are unconsciously triggered, and the person acting out isn't aware that their reaction is an unconscious one.

Growing up, I always spent school vacations at my aunt's house because my parents had to work. She and her husband argued all the time. The argument would start off with a light disagreement, and within seconds they were having a full blown fight. From what they were saying it didn't sound too serious, so I could never understand why they would end up wanting to kill each other. I hated going there, and I would beg my parents to let me stay at home alone but that wasn't possible. When I got older, my mom explained why Aunty Carol was so argumentative. Aunty Carol was my mom's cousin, and she was raised in an abusive household where fighting and arguing was all she knew.

It wasn't until I started studying emotional muscle memory that I understood why Aunty Carol was like that. Since aggression was stored in her subconscious, anytime she felt as if she was being attacked, she got defensive. From an outsider's perspective I didn't think my uncle asking her where she had put his white shirt was an attack. But because of what she had witnessed growing up in a controlling household where all hell broke loose if her dad couldn't find his shirt, as far as she was concerned, she *was* being attacked. When Aunty Carol started getting angry, the tops of her ears would go red, and that was the signal to my uncle that she was about to blow her top, and so he would blow his before she blew hers.

Sadly, Aunty Carol never overcame her anger issues and she went to the grave like that. But an effective way to improve our emotional state is to make a conscious effort to unlearn all the negative reactions that are stored in our subconscious mind. Dr. David Hawkins conducted a study about the frequencies that humans vibrate on. What he found was that the human body vibrates at a frequency of 0 to 1000+. Your vibrations depend on your emotional state and level of consciousness. Our emotions are like the frequencies of a radio channel. What do you do when you want to listen to a different channel? You change the frequency, right? Likewise, every emotion has a different frequency. The human body is made up of cells, the cells are made up of atoms and they are constantly vibrating. When you are playing the victim and blaming people for your circumstances, you are vibrating at a frequency of 30 out of 1000+. When you feel humiliated, you are vibrating at a frequency of 20. When you are in a state of bliss, you are vibrating at a frequency of 600. Take a look at the chart that Dr. Hawkins put together to get a better understanding of these different frequencies.

You will notice that the more positive the emotion, the higher the frequency. You will also find that when you are vibrating on a high frequency, you have more energy. However, when you are vibrating on a low frequency, you have less energy, and these are the energy drainers. The frequency you operate on is up to you, so you've got to choose which emotions dominate your life. If you've got kids, how do you want them to feel when they are around you? I know people who can't stand being around their parents because they operate on such a low frequency that they feel drained in their presence. Your frequency isn't just about what you say, it's about how you truly feel inside. People are capable of feeling who you are without you saying anything because we unconsciously tap into people's energy.

I'm sure you've heard of the saying, *"birds of a feather flock together."* Well, I'd like to change that to, *"birds of the same frequency flock together."* In other words, you attract people who are vibrating on the same frequency as you are. Let's say you've just had an argument with your partner, and you get in the car and drive into town. Because of the argument, you are in a really bad mood and on every corner, you seem to have a problem. People won't yield the right of way to you, someone takes your parking space, and you keep getting cut off on the road. Why is this happening to you? Because you are operating on a low frequency and so you are subconsciously attracting people who are operating on the same frequency as you.

On the other hand, I remember when I had just passed my driving test after failing three times. I was so happy that when I got out of the car and crossed the street, and there was a lady sitting at the bus stop, she immediately sensed that I was excited about something and she started smiling. We had a wonderful conversation before I got on the bus. On the bus, I had a lovely conversation with another woman, it was just happiness all around.

You can choose how you want to live your life. If you want to vibrate on a high frequency at all times, you've got to change the way you think. When you think happy thoughts, your emotions will follow. Just like the muscles in the body, you can strengthen your emotional muscles. Here's how:

Take Emotional Timeouts: All parents are familiar with putting their children in time out when they start acting up. Well, adults need time out too! Emotions are felt, and when you find yourself in a situation where anger, frustration or hurt start rising up, take some time out to process what has happened before reacting to a situation.

Forgive and Move On: One of the reasons why some emotions can be so damaging is because we refuse to let them go by holding on to unforgiveness. In Chapter 5 you read about trapped emotions. Sometimes we can be the cause of our trapped emotions because we are choosing to hold onto them and harbor resentment towards the person who wronged us. It may not even be a huge offense; someone might have pushed in front of you at the grocery store, you got angry, got in the car and complained about it to your partner. Later on that evening, you got on the phone and complained about it to your friends. The next day, you complained about it at work, and then again at the gym. Constant complaining about a situation means you are still harboring resentment towards a person. However, forgiveness means letting go of feelings of resentment and the need to get revenge on a person, accepting that the situation happened and moving on. If it was a friend or a loved one who hurt you, forgiveness doesn't mean that you start trusting them again and go back to the way things used to be. If you feel that the relationship can't be salvaged, cut them off, or keep the person at arm's length and get on with your life.

Don't Engage: When someone insults you or says something you don't agree with, the first thing you want to do is defend yourself or argue back. But not every argument is worth having.

People are going to form opinions about you and there is nothing you can do to control that. Additionally, people are not always going to agree with you, and there is nothing you can do to control that either. What you can control is how you respond to the offense. When you engage in fruitless discussions, you give people who don't deserve it your energy and your power. Think about it like this: it doesn't feel good to do 100 sit-ups at the gym, but it will do wonders for your body. Also, the pain is often unbearable during the workout, but you feel great afterwards. The same applies to emotional workouts.

Breathwork: If you are feeling that something is not quite right, don't self-medicate with mindless TV, shopping, alcohol or food. Allow yourself to experience the full emotion so that you don't bury it. Because as you have read, it will only resurface as something more destructive. You can bring yourself back to a calm and peaceful state through breathwork, and the following breathing exercise is great for re-centering:

- Sit in a comfortable position, put both hands over your heart and close your eyes.
- As you breathe into your heart, pay attention to how beautiful and powerful it feels. Spend some time focusing on that beauty and strength and feel the emotion of gratitude.
- Focus your attention on the situation that is causing you emotional distress and say it out loud. For example, *"I am feeling frustrated at the moment because I hate my job, and I've got a fantastic business idea, but I can't take action because I don't have the finances."*
- Keep your hand on your heart and listen to what it's trying to tell you.

- Connect to the power of your heart and mind and connect with the truth pouring from your higher self.
- Your higher self is the person you truly are but hasn't manifested yet. What would this person say to you?
- Your higher self isn't going to say anything negative, so only pay attention to the positive and breathe into those words. You might hear things such as, *"The only thing I need to focus on is doing my best," "The only thing I need to do is trust in myself." Or "In this situation, the only thing I need to remember is that only good will come out of it."*

Take your time with this breathing exercise and recognize that there are no right or wrong answers. The most important thing is to allow yourself to feel so that you can connect with the truth that is pouring into your soul from your higher self.

BECOME A RATIONAL THINKER

As I stated earlier in this book, a lot of people react to their emotions the moment they feel them. I believe that reactionary behavior is one of the main reasons why relationships fail. When there is a disagreement, instead of taking a break and thinking things through, one or both parties start screaming, shouting, insulting and whatever else comes with that moment of anger. Once those words are released, there is no taking them back, the damage has been done. Outside of the offense caused, there is zero joy in living in a household that is in constant turmoil. Becoming a rational thinker will make your life and the lives of those around you a lot easier.

We experience the world through our senses: sight, hearing, smell, touch or taste. Whatever sense is missing can be compensated for. For example, a blind person won't be able to experience the world through what they see, but they can do so with what they hear. All our senses are controlled by the brain, so when you touch something, the fingers send a signal to the brain to let it know that you've touched something. The same goes for any of your senses. An electrical signal travels up the spine to the brain and finds its way to the limbic system in the brain, the part that deals with the emotions. That message is then sent to the rational part of the brain called the hippocampus. In other words, we feel the emotion first, and then we rationalize it.

Therefore, in order to make a rational decision, you can't act immediately; you've got to give yourself some time. Let's say you've had a hectic day and you want to relax by going to the store to so some window shopping. You see a pair of shoes that you really like but they are way out of your budget. Without thinking, you go into the store and try them on. You fall deeply in love with the shoes and you decide to buy them. As you are admiring them in the mirror, your phone rings and it's your best friend Ashlee. Ashlee is well aware of your impulse buying, and when you tell her about the shoes, she reminds you that you can't afford them. Ashlee begins to reel off all your monthly expenses, and even though you are putting it on a credit card, you will end up paying for those shoes for the next six months. Now you start thinking with your rational mind, and by the time you've put the phone down, the shoes are back in the cashier's hand, and not only have you left the store, but you've also left the mall and gone home. At that moment, your best friend Ashlee got your rational mind to think about the consequences of such a big spend.

So, how do you make the transition from being a reactionary person to a rational thinker? Take a break. It's that simple. In the store scenario, if your friend hadn't called, you could have taken a break by walking around the mall a couple of times instead of going into the store to try the shoes on. During this time, your rational mind would have kicked in as you began totaling up your bills for the month. If you are at home having a discussion with your partner and you notice that emotions start running high, take a break and come back to the discussion when you've calmed down.

You can use this strategy at any time you feel emotional about a decision you've got to make. Don't react immediately, take a break, sleep on it if necessary and make the decision once you've thought it through.

Rational thinking is a skill that you should spend as much time practicing as possible if you don't want to react purely from your emotions.

Make a Commitment: Becoming a rational thinker is essentially about changing the way you think. It isn't going to happen overnight, and it's going to take some work. Your first step is to accept this challenge and commit to it. Changing the way you think is no different to going on a diet and exercise regime. If you are not prepared to put in the work, you won't succeed. Becoming a rational thinker is an opportunity for you to grow and develop and tap into a part of yourself that you didn't know existed.

What Are Your Cognitive Biases? For those of you who don't know, a cognitive bias is the process you take to simplify information, and these biases have a profound influence on the way you think about and see the world. One of the most important aspects related to rational thinking is confronting the cognitive biases you may have. A rational thinker comes to their own conclusions and provides a strong rationale to back up their arguments. You can determine your cognitive biases by paying attention to the things that you make assumptions about or jump to conclusions on. Once you have identified them, confront those biases by determining why you have them. What you will find is that they are unfounded.

Develop Your Own System: There are several systems you can put in place to improve your rational thinking ability. Some of these methods include:

- *Keep a Journal*: This journal is different to any other journal you might have. It's not about just releasing your emotions, but about evaluating and analyzing situations and events that have taken place. Write about your thoughts, your reactions, what you learned about yourself and the things you could have done differently for a better outcome. You should also include whether your behavior was rational or not.
- *Break Down the Problem:* If you run into a difficult problem and it makes you feel overwhelmed, take a step back, pause and break down the elements of the problem. Consider each element and write down why you are addressing them, identifying the overall purpose behind your concern. What question are you trying to answer, and what information do you need to find a rational solution to the problem?

Express Your Rational Self: A great way to practice rational thinking is to express your thoughts openly. You can start by speaking about your opinions to friends and family members.

Everyone has opinions, likes, dislikes and beliefs; the difference between a rational and a non-rational thinker is that rational thinkers are capable of explaining, supporting and being flexible in their thought process. When you are having a conversation about your opinions, do the following:

- Provide an explanation that is backed up with evidence to support your opinions. You can make your arguments stronger by collecting your evidence from an authoritative source.
- Think critically about the information or evidence that influences your beliefs or opinions.
- If new arguments or evidence is presented, be open to changing your opinion.

Join a Debate Team: A debate is a sensible argument in which both parties present evidence to challenge an opinion or belief. It is done in an intellectual and rational manner and it is not fueled by emotions. You can improve your debating skills by doing the following:

- Be prepared to defend, explain and articulate your opinions regarding an issue.
- Admit that the person/team you are debating with has made a good point and state that you had never thought about it that way before.
- Be open to listening to and accepting counter arguments that have solid reasoning. You can even ask how they came to their conclusion.

Don't Complain so Much: There is nothing wrong with expressing how you feel about a situation or letting someone know they've offended you in some way. However, when the majority of your time is spent complaining about the same thing, it is an indication that you are unable to think rationally. A rational thinker handles problems by evaluating the situation and coming up with a solution.

Practice Makes Perfect: It takes time, energy and effort to develop a more rational way of thinking. Therefore, you will need to practice this way of thinking often. To start, you will need to spend more time practicing, but it will eventually develop into a habit.

CONCLUSION

Emotions are powerful. They are the driving force behind everything you do. The road to good emotional health starts with learning how to manage your feelings and responses to those feelings. Flying off the handle feels good in the moment. But that feeling quickly disappears when you are cringing with shame and regret in the middle of the night. Emotional mismanagement is one of the key players in relationship breakdowns and that is not only because couples find it difficult to articulate their feelings. When emotions such as anger are acted upon without any rational thought, hurtful words are exchanged, and these words can't be taken back.

It is important to mention here that being emotionally healthy doesn't mean you bounce around on cloud nine all day. Life is full of challenges and no one is exempt from adversity, but the difference between an emotionally healthy and an emotionally unhealthy person is that they are in full control of their thoughts, feelings and behaviors. They can deal with the setbacks because they understand the power of perspective and know how to bounce back from difficult situations. Emotionally healthy people feel sadness, anger and stress, but they know when a problem is too big for them and when to ask for help. They know when to say no and don't try to carry the burdens of the world on their shoulders. Emotionally healthy people live balanced lives, and I am fully confident that you can achieve the same if you are willing to put the work in.

Unfortunately, there is no magic pill you can take to help you manage your emotions and maintain good emotional health. Achieving success in any area of life requires work. If you want emotional stability you've got to put the work in and develop a solid foundation that you can build on. Here is a quick recap of the steps you need to take to manage your negative feelings and maintain good emotional health:

Awareness: What are the things in your life that are causing you emotional distress? What are your triggers? Address these issues and put strategies in place to manage or change them.

Express Your Feelings: Burying your feelings doesn't serve you; no matter how well you ignore them, they will show up in other areas of your life either through an emotional outburst or sickness. Take some time out to process your feelings and when the time is right, express them in the appropriate way.

Manage Stress: We live in a fast-paced world and a lot of us operate on autopilot until we crash and burn. You can avoid this by managing stress effectively.

Create Balance: What are you doing too much of and what are you doing too little of? Are you spending too much time worrying about your problems and not enough time looking for solutions? Are you spending too much time at work and not enough time with friends and family? Are you obsessed with your physical health but neglecting your emotional health? Finding balance is essential to your emotional health.

Maintain Your Physical Health: A healthy body equals a healthy mind. Similarly, an unhealthy mind equals an unhealthy body. Eat well, drink water, get moving and sleep well.

Connect with Loved Ones: We are social beings and connection is important to us. Make time for friends and family, whether it's having dinner together, watching a movie or sitting down for a chat. Just make sure the people you are connecting with are good for your emotional health.

Find Meaning and Purpose: We only have a short time on earth to make an impact. Not only does the world need your gifts and talents, finding meaning and purpose will motivate you to become the best version of yourself.

REMEMBER...if you want to see results, you will need to put the work in.

I wish you all the best on your journey to emotional freedom!

THANKS FOR READING!

I really hope you enjoyed this book and, most of all, got more value from it than you had to give.

It would mean a lot to me if you left an Amazon review—I will reply to all questions asked!

Simply find this book on Amazon, scroll to the reviews section, and click "Write a customer review".

Or alternatively, please visit www.pristinepublish.com/emotionsreview to leave a review

Be sure to check out my email list, where I am constantly adding tons of value. The best way to get on the list currently is by visiting www.pristinepublish.com/empathbonus and entering your email.

Here I'll provide actionable information that aims to improve your enjoyment of life. I'll update you on my latest books, and I'll even send free e-books that I think you'll find useful.

Kindest regards,

Judy Dyer

Also by
Judy Dyer

Grasp a better understanding of your gift and how you can embrace every part of it so your life is enriched day by day.

Visit: www.pristinepublish.com/judy

REFERENCES

AAN, (2013) "Hold the diet soda? Sweetened drinks linked to depression, coffee tied to lower risk", Science Daily.

Acn, H. F. P. L. A. (2017). Unfuck Your Brain: Getting Over Anxiety, Depression, Anger, Freak-Outs, and Triggers with science (5-Minute Therapy) (Illustrated ed.). Microcosm Publishing.

Arab L, Guo R, Elashoff D. "Lower Depression Scores among Walnut Consumers in NHANES." Nutrients. 2019;11(2):275. Published 2019 Jan 26. doi:10.3390/nu11020275.

Berstein, G, (2020) "How to Use the Abraham-Hicks Emotional Guidance Scale".

Caltech (2015), "Microbes Help Produce Serotonin in Gut".

Covey, S. R. (1920). The 7 Habits of Highly Effective People (30th Anniversary Edition) (4th ed.). Simon & Schuster.

Cowen, A., Keltner, D "Self report captures 27 distinct categories of emotions bridged by continuous gradients" PNAS September 5, 2017.

Craft LL, Perna FM. "The Benefits of Exercise for the Clinically Depressed." Prim Care Companion J Clin Psychiatry. 2004;6(3):104-111. doi:10.4088/pcc.v06n0301.

Goleman, D. (1996). Emotional Intelligence Why it Can Matter More Than IQ Mass Market Paperback. 12 September 1996. Generic.

Grillo A, Salvi L, Coruzzi P, Salvi P, Parati G. "Sodium Intake and Hypertension." Nutrients. 2019;11(9):1970. Published 2019 Aug 21. doi:10.3390/nu11091970.

Gottlieb, L. (2019). Maybe You Should Talk to Someone: A Therapist, HER Therapist, and Our Lives Revealed (1st ed.). Houghton Mifflin Harcourt.

Harvard Health Publishing, (2019) "Sleep and mental health".

Harvard Medical Publishing, (2021) "Why stress causes people to overeat".

Hawkins, D.R, (2021) "Life's Energy Chart", Tao Aruba.

Huang Q, Liu H, Suzuki K, Ma S, Liu C. "Linking What We Eat to Our Mood: A Review of Diet, Dietary Antioxidants, and Depression." Antioxidants (Basel). 2019;8(9):376. Published 2019 Sep 5. doi:10.3390/antiox8090376.

Kranz S, Brauchla M, Campbell WW, Mattes RD, Schwichtenberg AJ. "High-Protein and High-Dietary Fiber Breakfasts Result in Equal Feelings of Fullness and Better Diet Quality in

Low-Income Preschoolers Compared with Their Usual Breakfast." J Nutr. 2017;147(3):445-452. doi:10.3945/jn.116.234153.

Nelson, B., & Robbins, T. (2019). The Emotion Code: How to Release Your Trapped Emotions for Abundant Health, Love, and Happiness (Updated and Expanded Edition) (Illustrated ed.). St. Martin's Essentials.

Noland, D., Drisko, J. A., & Wagner, L. (2020). Integrative and Functional Medical Nutrition Therapy: Principles and Practices (Nutrition and Health) (1st ed. 2020 ed.). Springer.

Ph.D., C. S. B., & Kirkland, S. (2014). Make Your Brain Smarter: Increase Your Brain's Creativity, Energy, and Focus (Reprint ed.). Simon & Schuster.

Ph.D, B. L. F. (2018). How Emotions Are Made: The Secret Life of the Brain (Illustrated ed.). Mariner Books.

Ph.D., E. P. (2007). Emotions Revealed, Second Edition: Recognizing Faces and Feelings to Improve Communication and Emotional Life (2nd ed.). Holt Paperbacks.

Schaefer SM, Morozink Boylan J, van Reekum CM, et al. Purpose in life predicts better emotional recovery from negative stimuli. PLoS One. 2013;8(11):e80329. Published 2013 Nov 13. doi:10.1371/journal.pone.0080329.

The British Psychological Society, (2012), "Putting a price on emotions", Research Digest.

USFDA, (2020) "Sodium in Your Diet".

US National Library of Medicine, (2019) "Stress Sensitivity and Reward Responsivity in Depression", Clinicaltrial.gov.

Wang J, Um P, Dickerman BA, Liu J." Zinc, Magnesium, Selenium and Depression: A Review of the Evidence, Potential Mechanisms and Implications." Nutrients. 2018;10(5):584. Published 2018 May 9. doi:10.3390/nu10050584.

Printed in Poland
by Amazon Fulfillment
Poland Sp. z o.o., Wrocław
02 August 2023

fd1e7600-f5f8-452e-96f6-32b957b8644cR02